THE GREAT

I

A

M

TWO SIDES TO

EVERY STORY

HIS   AND   OURS

THE GREAT
I
A
M

TWO SIDES TO EVERY STORY

HIS AND OURS

WANDA F. KENTY

ARPress
ILLUMINATING IDEAS
EMPOWERING VOICES

ARPress
45 Dan Road Suite 5
Canton, MA 02021

Hotline: 1(888) 821-0229
Fax: 1(508) 545-7580

Ordering Information:
Quantity sales. Special discounts are available on quantity purchases by corporations, associations, and others. For details, contact the publisher at the address above.

Printed in the United States of America.

ISBN-13:   Paperback   979-8-89330-756-6
                   eBook   979-8-89330-757-3

Library of Congress Control Number: 2024903751

CONTENTS

T his book is dedicated to the saved, the not yet saved Christian, and the atheist or anyone looking for a reason why they should believe in God. I was baptized and became a Christian at a very early time in my life. I would say approximately ten to eleven years of age. I didn't really know what I was doing. All I know is I was afraid of the devil and I didn't want to go to hell. I had heard God and Jesus Christ was the only way to stop that from happening. Church was called the house of God or God's house.

I wanted to meet Him. I wanted to know what He looked like, what He smelled like, and anything else I could find out about Him because I wanted Him to keep that devil away from me! Instead, I found a lot of people who looked a lot like me. There was a lot of music, singing, shouting, dancing, and screaming. A man came on the stage that looked a lot like me. He wore a long robe with a long, what looked like a tie, around his neck that he never tied up. He would talk a lot about God and Jesus Christ, and sometimes he would even scream! He kept a white handkerchief in his hand because sometimes he would talk so long, I guess he got hot a lot of the time and would have to wipe his mouth and face constantly.

Even with all of the music, the singing, shouting, dancing, and screaming, God or Jesus Christ never showed up! It's almost impossible to find a thing when you have no idea what to look for. That is the reason for this book. I believe if the church would have spent more time teaching about understanding who God is and what His relationship is to me, as well as mine to Him, I believe I would have caught a glimpse of Him long before now. So this is for those of you who have no idea who the Almighty Father God is and what His relationship is to you, as well as those who now have more than an idea of who the Almighty Father God is and the love expounding upon the knowledge of the who, what, when, where, why, and how the Almighty Father created, loves, and sustains us.

This book was written with you in mind and brought to fruition by the Holy Spirit through the Word of God from the Holy Bible.

This book is especially dedicated to my son, Paul E. Callender III (October 31, 1979–August 24, 2021).

PREFACE

November 14, 2017

I am a born again Christian! I confess this first and foremost because I have not always understood Christianity. To be totally honest, I kind of shied away from it. When I was a child I used to think that being a Christian meant being within a group of people who were special. I thought they were different than myself and that only an "extra" special kind of person could get in that group—a group that I would never be able to live up to. I was just a kid, and I already knew all the lies I told and candy I had stolen. I just knew God wouldn't want somebody like me anyway! I didn't believe I was good enough. I figured once I became a little older and got a little better at life, I could become a better person and maybe then God might notice me. Even though I went to church, I felt like I was on the outside looking in. There were people that went to church every Sunday in their (what people back in the day called) "Sunday-go-to-meeting" clothes. They would pull into the church parking lot in their nice, clean, polished car. The family would step out of that car immaculately dressed. The father with polished shoes, just like his car, wearing a pressed suit that appeared to never have been worn. His wife adorned with a beautiful hat, shiny stockings with matching purse and high heels. The son dressed to mirror his father with Bible in hand, and finally the daughter, dressed in frilly lace with anklet socks and white patent leather, strap-over shoes. She looked so happy and worry-free as her father kneels down and takes her up in his arms and carries her into the church. These were the people God wanted!

No worries. No problems. Just by looking at them you knew they had money to eat good every day and pay all their bills. They all loved each other. They obviously don't fight with one another because they go to church every Sunday! They probably went home to a house that was just as beautiful as their car! It must be something to live like that! I thought, "Wow! God must really love them to give them all that!"

"When I was a child, I spoke as a child, I understood as a child, I thought as a child; but when I became a man, I put away childish things" (1 Corinthian 13:11 NKJV).

I lived in the housing projects of Windsor Terrace in Columbus, Ohio, and when I did go to church, I attended Mt. Herman Baptist Church under Reverend S.R. Doughty Sr. on Windsor Avenue. My family oftentimes didn't have a car. My father didn't go to church. My mother would go when we could get a ride or when she didn't have to work. Sometimes we would walk. My mother dressed me nice for Sunday service. My body was clean. My hair was always combed. She polished my skin with Vaseline petroleum jelly, and in my sweater pocket, a quarter, for the collection plate. We didn't have a fancy home. Nevertheless, my mother always insisted it stayed clean. She didn't always have money to pay the bills but made sure we ate good most of the time, even if she didn't. My mother gave birth to eight children as seven survived. Of those seven, we fought and argued all the time! Well, maybe not all the time. A lot of the time would be the truer statement, but all of the time, fighting or not, we always loved each other.

When I reflect on my childhood church years, one thing always remained constant. Regardless how far in the past up to this present day, all the pretty families entered through the same doors that I entered. They sat in the same sanctuary, heard the same music, and were taught the same sermon. We were all different in that sanctuary. But when I grew up I realized God didn't love any of them more for all their pretty or me any less in all my ugly. He loved us for what we all needed, which was and still is His truth! His truth of who He really is. His truth about creating us in *their* image. His truth about how much He loved and prepared for us before He created us! And the truth of the gift of His intricate and infinite *life network* that He has freely given to each person or thing that has life.

I believe it is imperative that to even begin to truly believe the authenticity of the Almighty God, who is invisible, we have to be willing to accept and have faith in the abundant life that He has made visible. Therefore, having tangible proof of what we can see, we should be able to use that information to trace its origin, A root or truth that we all can accept and/or relate to. I guarantee it will lead us back to the beginning, "the invisible one." Remember, the genesis of any invention man has ever brought to fruition was birthed from the power of thought. The human inventor could see his thought within his own mind, but no one else could until he created it. Nevertheless, this process proves he is a real human who had or began his invention with a thought, and finally his thought is birthed into reality. So if the Almighty God devoted great thought and then created us and gave us the ability to create, why is it so unbelievable that God could not have the same power or ability He gave us, but on a much larger scale? Do you think it is honestly wise to believe that you obtain such a proven powerful ability and the ability originated from nothing? From nowhere! Or even worse, yourself!

The purpose or intent for this book is to offer insight to those who would like to venture further into the knowledge of Christianity but don't quite know where to start or maybe aren't clear or don't have a clue what it all means or what the Bible is telling them. I admit, the Bible is not the easiest book to understand. However, the Lord did say in Matthew 7:7–8, "Ask; and it will be given unto you. Seek; and you will find. Knock; and it will be opened to you. For everyone who asks, receives, and he who seeks, finds. And to him who knocks, it will be opened." So just know, if you want to know an answer, you have to start by asking a question. If the answer does not suffice or completely answer your question, continue the search until you find it. And if there are obstacles in your way, knock or pursue them until that door is opened for you, and you shall come into the answer(s). You will find it's a continual process, but the answers you find will be well worth it! Because, in the process of asking questions, you'll find the beginning of gaining knowledge. In gaining knowledge, you acquire understanding, and with understanding, if you ask the Lord for it, He will give you wisdom. And that, my friend, is a desire the Lord has for us all!

My prayer is that all who are looking for a relationship with the Lord will be willing to ask, seek, and knock until they receive their answer. It is my belief this root of truth in the one Almighty God, Jehovah, El Shaddai (the Almighty), must be established to be in agreement with and grow into what we are trying or willing to believe in. The seed of that root is faith. And planting that seed in the heart of any human willing to accept the real truth is my purpose in hope that the tree of life will take root in any and all who are willing to believe.

INTRODUCTION

My purpose for writing this book is to share evidence, which I have come to know and believe by revelation of the Holy Spirit in accordance with the Holy Bible, that God and His Word is absolute truth. Every word ever spoken from the breath of God into His creation leads back or returns to Him, full circle, and reveals added truths of His love and provision for us. His truth compounds! Every breath God expels into a new life form is example of His infinite life supply. My intention is to give witness to the truth that God is life and His life is also eternal. My intent further extends to proclaim that God is who He says He is. God can do what He says He can do and that God is in fact a trinity. Therefore, because He is, so are we! The Bible says we are made in "their" image according to "their" likeness (Genesis 1:26). That includes you! The amplification of the relationship between God and His creation is crucial. This has nothing to do with religion. It has to do with the reality of the one true God. This is information established through the Word of God and supported by the science of biology (the study of living organisms, which God created because without God, there would be no science) of where we come from, what we truly are, and how we are to fulfill His purpose in this gift of life that He alone has given each one of us. I will admit, before I arrived to the place I am in my walk with the Lord, I had questions. I had to make up my mind once and for all and ask God the questions that were of concern to me. Can you really do all that the Bible says you can do? Can

I really put my faith and trust in you? And if you really can do all these things, will you? And more importantly, will you do them for me?

It's funny how we become our own worst enemy thinking we, individually, are the worst people in the world. I thought God would not really want to help me because I believed I was the only one who really knew all the wrong I had done in this lifetime, and I mean all the wrong—that God probably would not want to accept me because I had been such a bad person. You know, it's odd how we seem to humanize God by thinking that He thinks and reasons the same as we do. We may think there are other people that have done greater things with their life and seem to be a much better candidate and more perfectly suited for God than ourselves. I thought God would probably bless them before He would me and bless them a whole lot more! But His Word tells me, "Trust in the Lord with all your heart, lean not on your own understanding. In all your ways acknowledge Him, and He would make your path straight" (Proverbs 3:5–6). So, keeping that thought in mind, I asked myself, "Why would the Bible say God could do all these things if He really couldn't do them?" Furthermore, if God is not who He says He is, then living would have absolutely no purpose and even more so, where would living come from? We would only be here for the time we could keep ourselves alive, and when our time is up, that's it! Game over! There would be no reason to believe in or love anyone or anything. No reason to believe in resurrection or afterlife. No reason for Heaven or hell, and no need for anyone or anything with the exception of food and water. Our existence would just be a huge self-served waste of time and everything else, for that matter. It would be as if we were sent here on a one-way trip to *this world's* fair, being given a ticket for one short ride on life, and when the ride of life stops, so do we. What is the sense in that! At some point I had to stop and ask myself, "How can this be true? How can this life we've come to know be so full of possibilities but it's purpose be so hopeless and empty?"

Therefore, if these things were found to be true, then God would be a liar and His presence, unnecessary. And if there are other gods or creators in our midst like Allah and Buddha, etc., why do we all look alike? Regardless of the fact that different race, creeds, and colors exist, why are all of our bodies and life cycles in the same exact order? Birth, life, and death. Flesh, bone, and blood. It seems to me that if there were different gods, there would be different types of beings, human and otherwise. There should be a type of *Star Wars* effect in the way we look, speak, and live. Also, there should be different colors and forms of blood and different locations of the brain, which acts as the nucleus for the entire body, and is situated at the head or Highest point of all bodies, with the addition of the blood whose only color on this entire planet is red, offers proof that we are all created equally. There is no difference. It is only our knowledge of good and evil that causes our differences and our death. The Bible says, "God Jehovah Elohim is the creator of life!" (Genesis 2:7). And eternal life (John 10:28)! The *breath of life* is what God blew into the nostrils of the God-handcrafted body of Adam. And if that God-given breath of life that went into Adam (a human flesh, you and me) is in fact the life seed, the living force of pure true energy that made Adam come to life, how is it possible for that God breath, that breath of life, to die?

Webster's Dictionary defines life as "The state of being alive." If something is defined as one thing, how can it also be defined as the opposite? Can an apple spend its lifetime being an apple, and then if someone takes a bite of or damages it, the apple becomes an orange? No, it cannot! However, apples and oranges were not created into existence by God, with the living spirit that He gave to man. Apples will always be apples, and oranges will always be oranges. Although they do not have life as humans have, but yes, once picked away from their life's source, they do die. That's why they are labelled as perishables. But within the Almighty God's creation of man, He made us special. He gave us His living spirit of life! How can the life of God do anything else except what it is designed or defined to do? It is life! It lives! I can conceive the fact that life can leave the body because life is spirit. Life is energy. Life is mobile. It can move in whatever direction it is guided. We must come to the understanding that life is alive. Flesh (material substance for instance, the apple and orange), by itself, is not alive.

Flesh is what God created from the earth and formed with His hand! Flesh also falls in the category of a perishable. From ashes to ashes, dust to dust (Genesis 3:19). We all know that on earth the spirit of life resides inside the blood, which is within the flesh. Life and flesh are created by and given from the same Creator. Also, life has to reside in the flesh if the flesh is to be active or be mobile. Only when the two combine do they become a living flesh. I will use an analogy which is far smaller than the power of the Almighty God but might offer a clearer picture.

We all know that to make a car function, it has to have a battery—a life source. No matter what other part (alternator, engine, starter, etc.) is working or not working, for that car to move it has to have power. Nevertheless, every internal mechanism of that car could be ruined, but the life of the battery is not affected! The battery (life) doesn't need the parts of the car to stay alive. It stands on its own. The parts definitely need the power of the battery to come alive. The battery can be removed from the nonworking car, but the battery itself is still live! If we were to put that same battery into any other car and that car having all of its vital parts intact, it will turn that car on. In other words, the battery will use or give the life that is within itself to sustain the car's mobility! And just in case you didn't know, every machine that was ever invented by man came into existence by God's blueprint of man! The only difference is manmade batteries do eventually die. But God, He is the true energizer, and He is not a rabbit! He is and gives eternal life! But to take hold of this concept, we have to start off by knowing that we are a *combination* of life and flesh.

Flesh—a supernatural God-created vessel! Vessels do break and wear out. In God's creation of man, the vessel is the body that life lives in.

Life—a supernatural energy that is alive internally and eternally within the breath of God, which activates the blood in the body. This cannot be touched, broken, aged, or ended by any vessel of flesh. However, just as life enters the flesh, it can and more than likely will be eventually removed because life is eternal, but flesh is not!

If you have ever been in a close relationship with anyone such as a family member or friend, and you've come to know and witness their true character, and someone falsely accused this person of being fraudulent, it would be seemingly fair to suggest that you would more than likely be compelled to give true witness or testimony on behalf of the person that you know is being falsely accused. God is my Heavenly father, and He is my friend. Although He doesn't need my or anyone else's approval of who He is, I am going to attest to His character anyway!

In the beginning of my walk with the Lord, I was still somewhat confused. Not as to whether I had made the right decision in choosing to follow Him, but more on how do I begin? I didn't have a plan. I didn't know what to do. I asked the Lord, "Where do I begin?" Then I heard a voice. I know you may be laughing right now or saying to yourself, "Oh boy, here it comes!" but seriously, I heard it as clear as the voice we all hear when we have hurt someone or done something we know in our heart was wrong. That same voice many of us have grown to ignore, but you and I both know we still hear it! At that point I was not willing to fully admit that it was the voice of God because it was far too early in my walk with God to truly say I knew His voice. However, this voice came as clear as fresh water saying, "Begin at the beginning." As far as I was concerned, that was the sound of good advice. So that's exactly what I did! I asked the Holy Spirit for guidance in gaining knowledge, understanding, and wisdom of the truths He would reveal to me, then I opened my Bible to Genesis 1:1.

But before I begin this endeavor, I must warn you, this is an attempt to collect a debt. Any information in this testimony will be used to collect that debt. The good news is this debt is not an attempt to complicate your life but an opportunity to renew it! It is not a debt you owe to someone else but one you owe yourself. A chance to be released from the curse of sin, which we all were born into through Adam, and choose for yourself whether or not for the remainder of your life you will eat from the tree of life, which is the Bible. The Word and walk of the King of kings, Jesus Christ, our Lord, Savior, and Redeemer, or remain in debt with only your knowledge of good and evil, your lucky rabbit's foot, and no chance in hell for redemption! But the best news is, if you choose correctly, *your debt has already been paid! Paid in full!*

The only thing you need to do is be willing to accept your receipt! As I begin, I would like to acknowledge our Lord, Father God, Jehovah Elohim, Heavenly Father, the Creator. I request the guidance of His Holy Spirit in the testimony of these truths.

Good morning, Heavenly Father God, Lord Jesus Christ, and Holy Spirit. Thank You for this beautiful gift of a brand-new day. Father, I thank You for all of the provisions You have made upon my life and the lives of all that You love and have created, past, present, and future. Father, I pray that Your Holy Spirit will lay foundation for this message presented. I pray that I may not speak anything that is not of Your will. I pray that these words to follow are not for self-gratification but for the glorification of You, Almighty God, who is worthy of all praise, the God I believe to be the one and only true God. Father, thank You for making me a part of your thought, for birthing that thought of me into fruition, for making me a part of Your purpose, and for providing me vision beyond my sight. Thank You for sending the life of Your Holy spirit. In the name of Jesus Christ, our Lord, Savior, and Redeemer, I say amen.

WELL WATER

I once traveled through life unfulfilled,
I never felt whole or content.
There was a need unmet, a thirst unquenched,
That followed wherever I went.

And that thirst began to grow, and before I could know,
I was taking whatever was given.
A slanderous remark, an indecent proposal,
Mistaken for making a livin'.

Then a rich man once said, "Follow me!
I'm sure to have just what you need!"
It made my head spin round and round.
It made my stomach bleed.

Then I came upon the house of a potter,
And behind it stood an old well.
The potter said, "Drink if you thirst after truth,
Drink and the truth shall prevail!"

As the potter brought forth his truth from the well,
It looked inviting and was cool to the touch.
As it entered my body, my soul was refreshed,
Not realizing I was receiving so much!

The more I could drink, the more I would,
Then felt guilty because of my greed.
But the potter said, "Ask and it shall be given,
And will include all that you need!"

For He is the Lord, and His word would be void,
If His well had been a retainer.
But it pours forth a truth that cannot be retained,
For He, Lord God, is the Container!

And now I am a vessel that's been filled with the truth,
From the well of the house of the potter,
And I'll venture the road where the thirsty abode,
As a friend with a cup of "Well Water."
And it will make you well!

Written by Wanda F. Kenty

CHAPTER 1
HIS STORY

In the beginning God created the Heavens and the earth. The earth was without form and void: and darkness was on the face of the deep. And the Spirit of God was hovering over the face of the waters. Then God said, "Let there be light." And there was light! And God saw the light, that it was good.

(Genesis 1:1–4 *The Spiritual Warfare Bible NKJV*)

I believe any of us who have read the Bible or has ever been the slightest bit curious about what the Bible has to say has read or have heard this passage at least once in their lifetime. But have we truly paid attention to the information God was giving us in the introduction of His story from the very beginning of creation? How God created and prepared this earth for man to inhabit in advance of His creation of man. Or could it be that we merely recite or memorize a biblical phrase that has been passed down throughout the ages? Personally, I do not believe many of us have given the introduction of His creation the true attention it deserves. In our story or opinion of God and whether or not He created us at all are far too many questions and different variables about who God is and how we were created. Questions such as, was the world really created by God? What is God? Does God even exist at all? (And I can't, for His life in me, even begin to understand how anyone could truly ask that question!) And if He does exist, why isn't He doing anything to make the world better?

1

Regardless to the barrage of questions about God, proof remains evident in the grace and majesty God has already shown throughout nature alone. Psalm 19:1 (NKJV), "The Heavens declare the glory of God; and the firmament shows his handiwork." But man is still not satisfied. However, the variety of beliefs and opinions lead to the belief that the majority of us believe in a higher power, but we just can't seem to agree on who or what that power is. Some ask whether He is the one Almighty God alone? Others ask, "Is He a trinity?" The Father, Son, and the Holy Spirit? I believe the question man really wants to ask is, "Is there truly a power out there greater than myself?" Therefore, let's put the book of Genesis under the microscope and amplify the validity of the unselfish love and undeniable preparation God put into the creation of the Heavens and this earth to ensure that His greatest creation, which is man, would have every need supplied to sustain and enjoy God's gift of life.

To gain full grasp of what you are about to read, you must first have full understanding of the difference between fiction and nonfiction. According to the *Merriam-Webster Dictionary*, fiction refers to something invented by the imagination or feigned. Nonfiction refers to literature based in fact.

The writings of the Bible, as well as the writings of this book, are based in fact and not of the imagination because these writings are about you and I. And if we are not real, who is reading and writing the books? And furthermore, why? In fiction, if a thought remains an image, it is as an unplanted seed that has no substance to give or sustain its life. But if that thought, which is the seed, is planted into a substance that gives it life (such as the earth or the brain which is created from the earth), that life is brought to fruition, which is the proof of nonfiction. That is reality. That, my friend, is you and I because the Lord God Almighty is "the Alpha and the Omega, the first and the last!" He has been around a lot longer than we have. In His nonfiction book, the Bible, The Lord God begins this book with His explanation of how His creation of earth and life began because of a fight that began, ended, and took place in Heaven.

For complete understanding of what the Holy spirit was revealing to me, He gave the instruction to give strict attention in the first paragraph to the order in which God the Father reveals this information. (The nouns in particular.)

Genesis 1:1 begins first and foremost with:

1. In the beginning "God!"—God is the Alpha and the Omega, the first and the last! God is the author and finisher of all that was ever created.

2. The Heavens—Although Heaven was already created, the Heavens were not actually created until the second day. But, God makes it known first and foremost that He is Almighty God and is on His throne in Heaven!

3. The earth—The Father lets us know that at this point, the earth has not yet been revealed. He said, "The earth was without form and void" (Genesis 1:2 NKJV). Although He is going to begin to create, His canvas is not clean. Before He gives form to the earth, there is something He has to make right in Heaven! It appears something tremendous is about to happen!

4. Darkness—God said, "Darkness was on the face of the deep." There's a quiet, a stillness you can almost feel. Something is not right! Something is either trying to hide or does not belong wherever this event is taking place, which I believe is in a body of water in the third Heaven, God's kingdom! I also believe it was in a body of water in Eden because Ezekiel 28:13 says that Lucifer, before he rebelled against God, was in Eden, the garden of God, but the earth had not yet been created. And Isaiah 14:13 said, "You said in your heart, I will ascend to the Heavens; I will raise my throne above the stars of God. I will sit enthroned on the mount of the assembly, on the utmost heights of Mount Zaphon." The stars of this earth are beneath God already. Therefore, the stars above God would have to be stars that are in the third Heaven, and the Eden of which the Bible spoke had to be in the lower region of the third Heaven,

because Lucifer said he would ascend to the Heavens (because earth is a replicate of Heaven, Heaven has to have a firmament also), Lucifer had to rebel in Heaven otherwise if he was the seal of perfection (Ezekiel 28:11). Why would God cast him down lest he rebelled? I say this because ordinarily, where there is God, there is no darkness!However, God tells us that darkness is present. Before the earth was created, this darkness did not have a chance! God had it all under control.

5. God's fifth mention is "the spirit of God," the almighty power of God among many other titles. He, like Almighty God, wears no flesh, and He also is very real. He is the power of God and the most difficult to describe. He is like the vine or vein of life and energy (in the Hebrew language, the Ruakh, which flows between the Heavenly father and His Son, Jesus Christ. The spirit of God is the living power system that unifies the Father and the Son. He is the third person of the trinity. The spirit of God is the body of God's power hovering, over the face of the—

6. waters—Over these waters The Holy Spirit is undoubtedly watching every move of that darkness. And last but nowhere in the vicinity of least—

7. Let there be light! The eternal word, not created but spoken into existence by the omnipresent, omniscient, and omnipotent voice of the spirit of God. A separation, a distinction, between light and darkness, day and night. "And there was light. And God saw the light, that it was good. God called the light day and the darkness He called night. And the evening and the morning were the first day" (Genesis 1:3–5).

Genesis 1:1 says, "In the beginning God created the Heaven(s) and the earth." I have not yet seen all of the Heavens which are mentioned at His beginning creation, but I am witness to the earth! The King James version of Genesis 1:2 says, "And the earth was without form and void." The Message Bible says, "First this: God created the Heavens and

Earth—all you see, all you don't see. Earth was a soup of nothingness. A bottomless emptiness, an inky blackness."

Foremost, may I say that I am not one to criticize anyone's description or attempt to shed light on the understanding of what the Bible is telling us. I also was searching for a better visual in understanding how all of this connects with God's creation of us. I asked the Holy Spirit for knowledge and understanding of what God was saying. It had not been made clear in my mind, the direct connection between God, the Heavens, the earth, and me. I had been asking the Holy Spirit for quite some time for the answer in a way in which I could conceive it. There was a strong desire in my heart to know! I believe that when the Holy Spirit knew I was ready to receive the answer, He gave it to me in a vision. He gave me an aerial view from the Heavens of this earth. Looking down, amidst the clouds I saw what resembled a large cell! A dark round ball or seed surrounded and immersed in an expanse of fluid. What is a cell? According to *Edition 16, Taber's Cyclopedic Medical Dictionary* by F. A. Davis, a cell is a mass of protoplasm containing a nucleus or nuclear material. It is the unit of structure of all animals and plants.

According to *Human Anatomy and Physiology Laboratory Manual, Cat Version,* by Elaine N, Marieb, fourth edition, "The Anatomy of the Composite Cell," the cell, defined as the structural and functional unit of all living things, is a very complex entity. In general, all cells have three major regions or parts that can readily be defined with a light microscope: the nucleus, the plasma membrane, and the cytoplasm. The nucleus is usually seen as a round or oval structure near the center of the cell. It is surrounded by cytoplasm, which in turn is enclosed by the plasma membrane. According to Wikipedia, in cell biology, "The cell is the basic, structural, and biological unit of all known living organisms. A cell is the smallest unit of life that can 'independently replicate' and are often called the building blocks of life." And, how can the cell independently replicate? Because that is how and what God created it to do.

Please allow me to be the first to admit that I am not thoroughly educated in the science field but have, for as long as I can remember, held an interest in it. Although I am not completely oblivious to science, my intent is not to present myself as any type of scholar or teacher. Because I do want to know and believe there is a true God, I have simply asked the Lord to give me answers to our connection to Him. The Holy Spirit instructed me to search for evidence to support what I believe He is revealing to me, accept what has already been proven and building from there. Therefore, I decided to search the Holy Spirit, as I conceived it saying, "Seek, and ye shall find." If the answer you seek is not found, then it is not of God because God is the creator of all things created, especially our science. That is not to say that because God is the creator of our science, the scientists are completely correct in all of their findings because many things are still unexplained. However, God is correct in all that He created. Because God is real and creation is evident, there should be a fingerprint of its origin. Therefore, having minimal knowledge of such a complex field of study may have been what allowed me the ability to perceive the commonality of, or connection to, the first structure of life in its most infantile state. However, it could be the exact opposite: the first structure of life in its most complex state of being purposing every work, great and small, as God created it to do. As this vision was introduced to me, seeing the earth (or what I thought was earth) as a cell made perfect sense. The following is a minute description of a cell's function so that you will have some idea of how the separation of light and darkness was presented.

In cell biology, according to wikipedia.org, the cell has two major parts. They are the nucleus and the cytoplasm. The nucleus (pi. nuclei, from Latin nucleus or nuculeus, meaning kernel or seed) is a membrane-enclosed organelle found in eukaryotic cells. On a molecular level in cell biology, the nucleus is a highly specialized organelle that serves as the information and administrative office of the cell. The protoplasm within the living cell excluding the nucleus is called cytoplasm, which contains all the vital micro-structure which is essential for the proper cell functioning. Cytoplasm is the fluid that fills the cells and serves several important functions. Cytoplasm holds the internal components in place and protects them from damage. It is a jelly-like substance that fills the cell. It is made up of mostly water and salt. (Just like the oceans and seas that surround and protect the earth and the sperm of the male that surrounds, protects, and becomes one with the ovum of the female.) Every living thing that God created is comprised of cells, cells of all different types and structures that enable different functions for and of the body of which it was created. God created the body of man from the earth. Those same cellular components that are abundant in the earth are in man.

In almost every cell in the human body a process called mitosis occurs. This process is crucial in all creation. According to *Human Anatomy and Physiology Laboratory Manual, Cat Version* by Elaine N. Marieb, fourth edition, "Cell division in all cells other than bacteria, consists of a series of events collectively called mitosis and cytokinesis. Mitosis is a nuclear division (division of the dense mass of the cell). Cytokinesis is the division of the cytoplasm (division of the fluid mass). So when mitosis and cytokinesis occur, a single cell goes through a phase where it splits in half. The nucleus or dense mass begins the separation, ending with the separation of the cytoplasm, or fluid mass, simultaneously forming two genetically *identical* cells known as daughter cells.

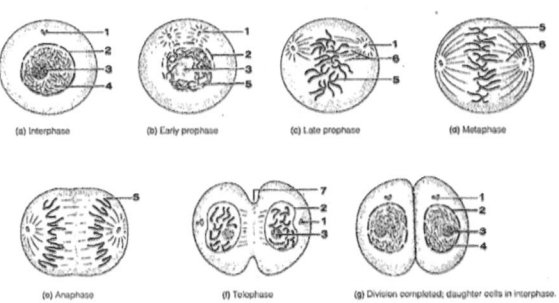

Therefore, out of one cell known as the 'mother' cell, it splits, separates, and becomes two identical cells. According to Wikipedia, mitosis and cytokinesis together define the mitotic (M) phase of an animal cell cycle—the division of a mother cell into two daughter cells genetically identical to each other. The process of mitosis is divided into stages corresponding to the completion of one set of activities and the start of the next." Therefore, out of one cell, which is currently known as the "mother," begins with a process of the mother cell splitting in half becoming two identical cells. Referring back to Genesis 1:1, where God created the Heavens and the earth, and using the vision the Holy Spirit gave to me, Heaven would had to have been the mother cell (the cell of which I thought to be earth because that's exactly what it looked like). Almighty God was on His throne in Heaven before He began to create. Heaven was already established. Somewhere in Heaven, a body of water held darkness that was on the face of the deep. "Then God said, 'Let there be light!' And God saw the light, that it was good" (Genesis 1:3–4). That *light* the Father spoke into existence was the light and force that split Heaven into two identical worlds: Heaven and the earth! I have heard in different sermons of things in Heaven that are identical to or possessing things that we can identify with here on earth or that Heaven and earth mirror each other. If we can identify with the things in Heaven, then Heaven had to pass the image onto earth. Earth was, at one time, inside or a part of Heaven itself. (I will give explanation of that later.) There are mentions of seas, thrones, jewels, lamps, thunder, voices, and even rainbows in Heaven (Revelation 4:6). There are mentions of houses and mansions, etc. in Heaven. We, as creations of our Father who is in Heaven, are well aware of what all of these things are although none of us have yet seen Heaven. Jesus told His disciples, "In My Father's house there are many mansions; If it were not so, I would have told you. I go to prepare a place for you" (John 14:2).

After God spoke the word *light*, there was no further mention of darkness being on the face of the deep. God divided the light from the darkness (Genesis 1:4). God called upon *emanated* light to separate the darkness. The light that God called upon could not have been the light from the sun because God did not summon its existence until the fourth day. At this point, the earth was still without form. According to *The Webster Student Dictionary and Thesaurus,* the definition of form as a verb is "1) To make, to cause to take shape. 2) To come into existence." Genesis 1:2 says, "The earth was without form. The earth was not of its own: Just remember, the fact that the earth is mentioned with Heaven in the beginning although it does not physically exist means that it is already real. God just has not revealed it 'yet.'"

The darkness which was upon the face of the deep was cast out of or separated from Heaven, as God created from the separation a world of its own that He called earth as earth was separated from or became the daughter cell of Heaven. Although Heaven and earth may not have been synonymous in their being revealed, the Father God and His angels were and still are in the third Heaven and man is on this earth with Satan, the darkness, the darkness that was upon the face of the deep.

I know some of you may be thinking this sounds a little unethical, but if you can allow yourself to bear with me for a little while longer, you may also witness this vision come into full view. In all things God is omniscient, omnipotent, and omnipresent and has never been proven untrue. Upon the entrance of light, God said, "Let there be a firmament in the midst of the waters the waters in Heaven where the darkness was, and let it divide the waters from the waters" (Genesis 1:6). Heaven, being the mother cell during mitosis, the cytoplasm (or waters) and nucleus (being Heaven) experienced the God-summoned light in its core that splits and causes complete separation from each other creating the space or firmament between the two daughter cells. Hence: "The Big Bang!" For an example, imagine you are frying an egg. Using a spatula as the light, placing it in the center of the egg and moving one side to the left or right, or pulling outward from the center of the egg, you would end up with a visual interpretation of mitosis: the mother cell (the whole egg) with a firmament or space dividing it. (In the true separation there would be two whole cells, not two halves.) God divided the waters which were under the firmament (division) from the waters which were above the firmament and it was so. This tells me that the daughter cell that would become known as earth is below the Heavens, which we all know and see. Because Satan was thrown down, where else could he have landed? God said darkness was on the face of the deep as well. Genesis 1:1–4 clearly states that the earth was without form and void; meaning, at that moment, earth was absent. There is mention of a body of water. It mentions that the spirit of God was on the face (or top) of the water and darkness was on the face of the deep (or bottom part of that same body of water).

"And God said, 'Let there be light.' And there was light. God saw the light, that it was good." God *divided* the light from the darkness. The light cut away the darkness. When that happened, God, Heaven, the face of the water, the spirit of God, and the light were all on the upper half of the division. Darkness was on the bottom. "And God said, 'Let there be a firmament in the midst of the waters. Let it divide the waters from the waters'" (Genesis 1:6). We now have two separate bodies of water from that one body of water. God divided the water, which was below the firmament (or separation), away from the waters that were above the firmament. He called the firmament Heaven. (God separated the Good from the bad.) So the evening and the morning were the second day. Genesis 2:4–5, "This is the history of the Heavens and the earth when they were created. In the day that the Lord God made the earth and the Heavens. *Before* any plant of the field was in the earth. *before* any herb of the field had grown."

"Then God said, 'Let the waters under the Heaven(s) be gathered together into one place, and let the dry land appear'; and it was so. And God called the dry land Earth, and the gathering together of the waters He called seas. And God saw it was good" (Genesis 1:9–10 The Spiritual Warfare Bible).

Now the earth is no longer without form and void. The earth is now established. In Genesis 1:1, the Bible says, "The earth was without form and void," because it had yet to be pulled out of or gone through the process of mitosis from Heaven. He who would become the prince of darkness was there in Heaven, and God exposed him by calling the everlasting light of Himself into the midst. "And God saw the light, that it was good: God used the light to separate or cut away the darkness. God called the light Day Heaven void of darkness, and the darkness He called Night earth revealed, because God also knew that this is where the darkness was. The place where Satan now lives. So, the evening and the morning were the third day." God saw the light, that it was good. He said nothing about the darkness.

There are scriptures from the Bible regarding three realms of Heaven. The first Heaven is our immediate atmosphere that is visible to the eye, the space where clouds form and birds fly. This space God referred to as the firmament (Genesis 1:6–8). The second Heaven is where the sun, moon, stars, and galaxies were set. (Outer space! Also a part of the firmament.) "The Heavens declare the glory of God; and the firmament shows His handiwork" (Psalm 19:1). All of what is created by God that is above our head is God's firmament. The third Heaven is said to be "beyond the space and stars." This is where God and the holy angels (and hosts) and spirits of just men dwell. The waters that God called above the firmament were the waters separated from the darkness of the deep water. This water is returned to "the Heaven of Heavens" (which I believe to be the mother cell).

> Praise the Lord! Praise the Lord from the Heavens; Praise him in the heights! Praise Him, all His angels; Praise Him, all His hosts! Praise Him, sun and moon; Praise Him, all you stars of light! Praise Him, you Heavens of Heavens, and you waters above the Heavens! (Psalm 148:1–4)
>
> I know a man in Christ who fourteen years ago—whether in the body I do not know, or whether out of the body I do not know, God knows—such a one was caught up to the third Heaven. (2 Corinthians 12:2)

The third Heaven is the eternal home where all who believe and commit their life here on earth to Jesus Christ will dwell (John 3:36). Anyone that is not willing to commit their life to Christ will not see the third Heaven for Christ said, "But whoever denies Me before men, him I will also deny before my Father who is in Heaven" (Matthew 10:33). That statement makes perfect sense. If you deny, won't accept, or are unwilling to acknowledge the authority of a person while you are in their home, why would you expect them to let you live in their house if you are not going to respect them or abide by their rules? We experience that with our own children and family members today. To allow someone you love and welcome to live in the home you have established, but they deny you and your will to be done in your house, that should not be tolerated by anyone. That is blatant disrespect!

That is exactly what happened when Lucifer was a member of God's family in Heaven. Ezekiel 28:11–17 said Lucifer (who later became Satan) was one of if not the most beautiful of God's angels, "the anointed cherub." He had the love of God. But that was not good enough for Lucifer. Isaiah 14:12–15 says he turned on God. He wanted to throw God off His throne, in God's own house! Lucifer was the first and only to bring jealousy and confusion in God's house and in the face of the inhabitants of Heaven. Lucifer was not seduced by anyone or ate from any tree to learn this jealousy. This jealousy was birthed from within himself. That is why he is known as the father of lies. Satan gave birth to something new, something never produced and never before introduced, to the body of Heaven that was not, is not, and never will be a part of God or Heaven. Satan wanted God to serve him! As you've seen, God was not about to let that happen, so God threw Lucifer down from Heaven. Lucifer also had followers. One-third of the stars of Heaven is what the Bible quoted. (You know how some just can't resist a pretty face!) Well, God could! And as we all know, Satan is not beautiful anymore! The Almighty threw his followers down right along with him (Revelation 12:3–9).

This is what establishes the theory of the vision of the cell and cellular mitosis. Because God is true, Heaven is real and it is pure. Regardless of the depths of Heaven, it should be pure and without spot, from the bottom of Heaven to the top (if there is such a thing). In the Heaven of Heavens, Lucifer displayed rebellion in the house of the Lord and somehow ended up trapped in the waters or sea of the Almighty God. Lucifer was that darkness on the face of the deep. I believe that when God said, "Let there be light!" that light cut through that water in Heaven, creating a division, a seal over that darkness that was on the face of the

12

deep, and God took the light of His foot and kicked Lucifer out! Threw Lucifer down. Separated Lucifer and anyone and or anything that had any affiliation with him from God's house. (The foot part, that's my version. Bear with me. God isn't through with me yet!)

Secondly, as the Bible speaks of God creating the earth, that is exactly where Satan and his followers landed. We are all witness to this fact with all of the evil displayed in this world. But before I continue, let me state for the record, what I am about to say is my own personal belief. This is not in the Bible, but it won't change anything the Bible states, but upon entering into the mention of God's creation of earth it is my belief that God definitely created the earth. I also believe that Heaven and earth are from the same making. But I don't believe the generation on this earth from Adam until now was the first or only generation that inhabited this earth. There has been too much evidence of previous life that is proven to be older than the life of the first Adam of our generation. Evidence of bones of Neanderthal and dinosaurs and such that are not mentioned in the Bible gives reason for my belief of this. And yes, I do believe God created them also. But I also believe they are not mentioned in the Bible because they don't pertain to this Adam (or Adamic) generation. However, the sufficient evidence of generations older than Adam that lived on this earth provides an open door for Satan, the deceiver, to incite doubt and challenges of evolution in an attempt to take away the credibility of God's creation from its beginning. But God is who He says He is and will always have the last word. The Alpha and the Omega! Therefore, I do believe that Satan was thrown out of Heaven long before our generation of Adam.

God said, "Let the earth bring forth grass." And the earth obeyed. The grass for one purpose provides a covering for this newborn earth's protection. And the earth brought forth grass, the herb that yields seed according to its kind, and the tree that yields fruit, whose seed is in itself, according to its kind. And the trees the Lord provided allows purification of the oxygen of the air we breathe. And God saw that it was good. So the evening and the morning were the third day. (Genesis 1:11–13)

Then God said, "Let there be lights in the firmament of the Heavens to divide the day from the night: and let them be for signs and seasons, and for days and years: and let them be for lights in the firmament of the Heavens to give light on the earth," and it was so. Then God made two great lights; the greater light to rule the day, and the lesser light to rule the night. He made the stars also. These lights also provide nourishment to the earth. The Lord God constantly makes provisions for all that He created.

God set them in the firmament of the Heavens to give light on the earth and to rule over the day and over the night, and to divide the light from the darkness. And God saw that it was good. So the evening and the morning were the fourth day.(Genesis 1:14–19)

Therefore, as it is explained on this fourth day, the greater and lesser lights that were made could not have been the same light in Genesis 1:3, which was spoken into existence on the first day. Day did not exist until after the light was summoned. Genesis 1:3–5 (NKJV Spiritual Warfare Bible) said, "Then God said, 'Let there be light'; and there was light. And God saw the light the light that He had just called upon, that it was good; and God divided not the day from night but the light, which is Heaven, from the darkness the darkness that was on the face of the deep. God called the light Day with a capital D, and the darkness He called Night a capital N. So the evening and the morning were the first day." Therefore, on the first day, God kicked Lucifer out of Heaven in the event of creating the first day of the light.

Now, just as a note, from the first day in Genesis 1:1 to the fourth day, God used these days to create the Heavens, the earth, and the firmament. Within these four days when God spoke, "Let there be," there was! No other words followed the Lord's speaking, and what He spoke was summoned. Let there be light, a firmament of Heaven, dry land naming it earth, and the waters naming them seas. Everything within the creation of the Heavens and earth alone is spoken into existence from God's permission, through the spirit of God. "Let there be!" Then on the fourth and fifth day:

God said; "Let the waters abound with an abundance meaning a lot, a whole lot of living creatures, and let birds fly above the earth across the face of the firmament of the Heavens. So God created great sea creatures and every living thing that moves with which the waters abounded according to their kind, and every winged bird according to its kind. And God saw that it was good. And God blessed them saying, "Be fruitful and multiply, and fill the waters in the sea, and let the birds multiply on the earth." So the evening and the morning were the fifth day.

Then God said, "Let the earth bring forth the living creatures according to its kind; Cattle and every creeping thing according to its kind"; and it was so. And God made the beast of the earth according to its kind, and everything that creeps on the earth according to its kind. And God saw that it was good. (Genesis 1:20–25)

According to *The Collins English Dictionary*, the word *according* is defined as "in proportion or in relation to" (its kind). Therefore, everything that God allowed to exist between His creation of the Heavens, the earth, and the firmament were created once and for all time. What appears the fourth and fifth days appear to be restorative because they are called to be "according to its kind." God summoned a thing and gave it instruction to be according to its own kind. His creation of man (Adam) is what God allowed to be brought forth according to "their own image"—the image of the Trinity. "according to image of God." "According to its own kind" was not spoken upon the creation of man. On the fourth and fifth day, whatever these lives are in proportion or relation to, according to their kind, had to have a date or time of origin in another day and time to have something follow in or be in accordance with or to it. (This is another reason I believe the earth is older than Adam. Just a note.)

Up to this point God has spoken everything into existence. Then in Genesis 1:26–27, it says, "And God said, 'Let us make man in our image, after our likeness: and let them have dominion over the fish of the sea, and over the fowl of the air, and over the cattle, and over all the earth, and over every creeping thing that creeps on the earth.' So God created man in his own image, in the image of God created he him: male and female created he them."

Genesis 1:31 (NKJV), "And God saw everything he had made, and indeed it was very good. So the evening and the morning were the sixth day." All of creation was complete.

CHAPTER 2
THE CREATION AND DESTRUCTION OF MAN

"Thus the Heavens and the earth were finished and all the host of them. And on the seventh day God ended His work which He had made: and He rested on the seventh day from all His work which He had made" (Genesis 2:1–2). This statement does not indicate that God stopped being God because He rested. It simply means that God was finished with the process of creation. There was nothing else the earth would need to exist. "And God blessed the seventh day and sanctified it: because in it He had rested from all of the work which God created and made" (Genesis 2:3).

This is God's statement that His creation is finished. Any and all things that needed to be created to sustain all forms of life on earth were complete. Nothing needs to be added or subtracted from what He created from the beginning of His works to the end of this earth's time. Just as a note, the fourth verse of the second chapter of Genesis (KJV) makes a definitive statement that says, "These are the generations of the Heavens and of the earth when they were created in the day that the Lord God made the earth and the Heavens." This verse is one that increases my belief that there was pre-Adamic life on earth. If the generation of Adam was interrupted and regenerated with Noah or even the ice age, there very well could have been prior generations of beings created by God but maybe not created in God's image before Adam. It would give explanation to the difference in the age of the earth and Adam. However, the creation of man (Adam), being created in the image of God, is our main focus.

As previously stated in Genesis 1:26 (KJV), "And God said, 'Let us make man in our own image, after our likeness.'" Genesis 1:27 goes on to say, "So God created man in His own image, in the image of God He created him: male and female He created them. And the Lord God formed man from the dust of the ground and breathed into his nostrils the breath of life; and man became a living soul." I have always been told by different pastors and people of the church that this verse applies to the fact that we were created in His image because we were all created with a body, soul, and spirit. Although I believe that to be true, I believe God's meaning of how we are created "in their image" goes a lot deeper than that. First of all, God said, "Let us make man in our own image, after our likeness." That can only mean in the image of the Trinity: the Father, the Son, and the Holy Spirit. That is how the Almighty identifies Himself. If that were not so, God would have more than likely said that statement in singular form. The Father is not one solid idol or material piece that you can hold in your hand or place upon a pedestal. Genesis 1:27 says, "So God created man in His own image the Trinity or wholeness of Himself in the image of God He created him," which means the Creator created man with the ability to also procreate. "Male and female He created them." Just as God created the Heaven with the ability to procreate *Mother* Earth. He also gave man the ability to procreate man. He pulled from the earth the ability to procreate male and female. The ability of male and female to procreate! The holy power of procreation.

What makes God a whole unit is because He is the Almighty Father, His only begotten Son, Jesus Christ, Emmanuel, "God with us," who is pulled out of the Father, and the spirit of God, the life and power within that binds the Almighty Father and Son. While God, being still in Heaven, His throne home, holds the totality of all of the Heavens and earth within it, waiting to be called out and at His will. Afterward, He created man and at the same time awarding man a part of the inheritance of creation from the Father, the ability to bring forth or procreate the male and female beings within the makings of His mankind to multiply human life upon the earth.

A new beginning!

In Genesis 1:1, where God created the Heavens and the earth, I spoke about a form of mitosis where earth was pulled out of Heaven and formed two daughter cells. Well, here we are again with another form of mitosis involving God's creation of man and how God gave man the ability to procreate. In Genesis 1:27, it states, "So God created man in His own image, in the image of God He created him the man. Male and female He God created them the man, who has been given the ability to make both male and female children." The female has nothing to do with whether or not, in pregnancy, the child will be a male or a female. At this time, I don't believe God was saying He was creating two people at the same time, male and female. It is seemingly obvious that the woman came on the scene much later. Therefore, woman, at this point, was much like earth in the beginning, "void and without form," waiting to be called or pulled out. Genesis 2:7 (KJV) says, "And the Lord God formed man of the dust of the ground, and breathed into his nostrils the breath of life; and man became a living soul." The mention of the woman was not until Genesis 2:22.

A lot of time had passed between these verses. However, verses 20 to 21 of Genesis 2 (KJV) says, "And Adam gave names to all of the cattle, and to all the fowl of the air, and to every beast of the field; but for Adam there was not found an help meet wife/match for him. And the Lord caused a deep sleep to fall upon Adam and he slept: and God took one of his Adam's ribs and closed up the flesh instead thereof." Just as in Genesis 1:6 (NKJV), "Then God said, 'Let there be a firmament separation in the midst of the waters and let it divide the waters from the waters." From the one body of Heaven, Heaven and earth was formed. From the one body of man formed from the earth, man and woman were created.

According to *The Anatomy and Physiology Laboratory Manual* by Elaine N. Marieb, RN, PhD at Holyoke Community College, a human cell consists of forty-six chromosomes which make twenty-three pairs. In males and females the first twenty-two are similar across both genders and are known as autosomes. The last one pair (the twenty-third) is known as the sex chromosome and makes all the difference. There are two sex chromosomes. The sex chromosome of the female contains two X chromosomes, while that of the male contains (X) female and (Y) male chromosome. That is why the Bible says, "Male and female He God created them" (the male, with both male and female chromosomes). The presence of this last chromosome pair determines the gender of a newborn. It was the X chromosome that the Lord took from Adam's rib (through some form of mitosis, because man still carries an X chromosome) to make the female (Eve). Therefore, the female is created as the female - the X gender. Because of the process of this making, it is the male that determines the gender of a newborn. The female sex chromosome is comprised of two X chromosomes. If during sex the male donates an X chromosome, the newborn will be female because they are all the same chromosome. If the male donates a Y chromosome, the newborn will be male because the Y chromosome, which is the male chromosome, will be the dominate chromosome because man was created first. For this reason, Almighty God was able to make woman from Adam's rib from the X chromosome within the blood cell in the bone marrow. A trinity! Two X's plus one Y equals to male trinity chromosomes. Three X chromosomes equals to female trinity!

Because gender can be determined through bone marrow, it seems only logical that God would use a rib because it is the only part of the skeleton with ample supply. With exclusion of the facial and skull bones, most others come in pairs or mirror each other excluding the hyoid which is singular and needed in each adult individual. The fact that the bone used to make woman was "taken out" of man is similar to earth being taken out of Heaven. The earth mirrors Heaven. Woman mirrors the man. They are both of the same making within their own unit as they are also opposites.

For instance, the third Heaven, God's house, there is complete obedience. On earth, a God-created home where Satan was thrown down, there is complete disobedience. The male stature is masculine, while the female is feminine. The male chest is muscular inside the body, while the female breast is muscular outside of the body. Male sex organs are outside the body. Female sex organs are inside the body. But they are both of their same making or makeup. As we know for fact, in male and female there is a balance! That's why we fit. It's like hand in glove. When you put your hand into a glove, it is like hand in hand. When you take out the hand and the glove turns inside out, it is hand and hand. Either way, nothing is disturbed or distorted. It is whole as a man (outside). It is whole as a woman (inside). It becomes one whole unit when we come together (preferably in marriage). We become one whole life unit with the ability to create another whole human that mirrors us. God's purpose! Trinity! Father, Son, and Holy Spirit! God in Heaven, who is the Father, ruler of the Heaven's and the earth, and the order of God's trinity is Father God, the man and the woman. Fulfilling God's purpose. Wherever God's purpose is fulfilled, you will find a trinity. This is why God says in Genesis 2:24, "Therefore a man shall leave his father and mother and hold fast to his wife."

For this reason, I agree homosexuality is a sin. If God did not purpose it, He will not bless it! God instructed His creation to be fruitful and multiply. Man was created to follow God's instruction. God created all mankind. God loves all mankind. But the fact of the act within the choice of mankind within homosexuality is what the Lord despises. But God will always love and forgive the person if he or she wills or wants to turn from their way and repent. God's purpose for man was not for man to be obedient to himself. God's purpose for man was to be obedient to his Creator, to continue a life that increases the light of man to fight the darkness of sin on this earth. Two of the same sex cannot fulfill that purpose. There can only be fulfilled self-gratification through their individual choice of sexual preference. Nothing else can be achieved. Two of the same gender together will forever and always be two. They can never become one or achieve unity because there is nothing to unite. There is no balance. No wholeness. The other component will always be missing. There would be the absence of fertilization. No ability to multiply. No ability to honor the Creator with a contribution to life for His kingdom. No other purpose in life can be achieved other than maybe serving other people, but that purpose can only be for the purpose of self-gratification or self-praise, because there would be nothing higher that you honor enough to offer the praise to. There is no glorification to our Creator. Almighty God created us in this earth because He knows it is inhabited by Satan. God was the one that kicked him down here. But because God is the Creator that gives and sustains life, He also gave life to us to stand with Him in righteousness. We are to be an army of God's creation on this earth made to stand in the face of Satan and his army to proclaim and glorify the name of the Almighty God, Jehovah Elohim, Creator of all the Heavens and the earth and all of creation. "Heaven is God's throne and the earth is His footstool" (Isaiah 66:1 NKJV). He is even the Creator of Lucifer (Satan) before he was thrown out of Heaven. He was then, is now, and forever will be the Almighty God! Mankind must seek His kingdom first (Matthew 6:33 KJV). When we come to know how life and order is done in Heaven, God's man on earth will learn the order of the army of God. He will learn how to wear the armor of God and how to fight for the kingdom of God, that we may have life and order on earth the same as it is in Heaven. "Thy will be done on earth, as it is in Heaven" (Matthew 6:10 NKJV).

This life here on earth is an orientation for the service God will call us to do in Heaven. If you have been given instruction of a job or position and you do not or will not take the instruction and follow the procedure to acquire the position, how can you expect your name to be called?. Regardless of whether or not you know or believe, the flesh returns to dust, but the spirit life of God is given from God. Remember, Satan was kicked out of Heaven because he tried to turn God's house into what earth is right now. And all of mankind here on earth who do not live in obedience of our Creator, Almighty God, gives Satan hope and determination to keep up his fight. Because whether or not you know this or accept it, if you are not for God or do not admit that you choose or receive Him as your personal Lord and Savior, then you are against Him! You may not want to be, but you are. There is no in-between. You have no say-so in the matter!

In Heaven, there is God and God's way only. But Satan came along and "created or brought out of himself a different kind of life" or another way of living. Now there are two ways of living: a good and righteous way and an evil and very unrighteous way, some of which we are experiencing right now. "But God, knowing their thoughts said to them: 'Every kingdom divided against itself is brought to desolation, and a house divided against a house falls'" (Luke 11:17). The good and perfect way is not saying that you can't have fun and enjoy friends or have a life and money, but to have these, and have them more abundantly, knowing and not being ashamed to proclaim that it is by the grace of God that you receive it. Psalm 35:27 says, "Let them shout for joy and be glad; Who favor my righteous cause; And let them say continually, 'Let the Lord be magnified; Who pleasures in the prosperity of His servants.'"

However, these are the only two choices we have. There is no limbo. There is no straddling the fence. Like it or not, we are bound by what our ancestors have done in the Old Testament. In living by the law(s) of the commandments, there was still no sure way back to God. But because a new testament has been afforded us by the blood, grace, and mercy of the Lord Jesus Christ, our Savior, we can break that tie that binds us. God wants you to ask for His guidance. God wants you back because you truly are His child. Man and woman create the body of flesh and bone, but Almighty God gives them life.

Satan does not want you to ask the Lord to come into your life because Satan knows if you don't ask the Lord (because the Lord has to be invited), you automatically remain his because our first grandparents took into their mouths and swallowed his seed, and Satan's evil is our gift of his inheritance. You are uncovered. Choosing life between God and Satan is like a life insurance policy. Either you're covered (by the blood), or you're not! Satan doesn't ask. He will take it! Satan is one of those who won't wait for an invitation. He will come to the house party uninvited and take over your whole house. However, Satan can never defeat the Almighty God. God is waiting for us, and He can save as many of us that are willing to be saved. But in Satan's war day by day, he is making this world a more dark and corrupt place in which to live so that those who may be or are truly looking for the light of life will have a much harder time finding it!

As for the woman God made, Genesis 2:22–24 (KJV) says, "And the rib, which the Lord God had taken from man, made he a woman and brought her unto the man. And Adam said, 'This is now bone of my bones, and flesh of my flesh: She shall be called woman, because she was taken out of man.' Therefore shall a man leave his father and his mother, and shall cleave unto his wife: and they shall be one flesh."

As man and wife physically become one flesh and the sex chromosomes have been applied, we arrive again at trinity. For this reason, the term Holy Matrimony is applied. Being that God made woman for and from man, they have God's blessing to come together and create other human beings to continue life and increase the army of the Lord. The term "HOLY" is applied because sex, which I believe to be one of God's most beautiful gifts, is a blood covenant. When a man and woman repeat marriage vows, the vows imply a commitment from both individuals to God and before a witness or witnesses of faithful commitment to each other only.

Marriage is a threefold commitment and covenant. The man and woman stand in the presence of God and confess their love to each other, asking for God's blessing upon their union. Threefold covenant. Trinity! After the marriage is consummated, the bride, being a virgin, will have a show of blood, which fulfils covenant and implies surrendering or sacrifice. Therefore, young men and women, please give considerable thought to your virginity, for it is an invaluable gift unto the Lord and your husband or wife. It is one of few gifts that is Holy and that you can only give once.

God is so amazing! When God made man in His image, God truly opened Himself for us to see what we truly mean to Him as well as why He created us in His image. When God gave the command to "be fruitful and multiply," I don't know if we truly realize the gift He gave us in creating our bodies with the built-in ability to do such a great and marvelous thing—the ability to recreate man! In today's world, this process is repeated so often in and outside of marriage. I don't believe we realize the wondrous beauty of this truly exceptional gift from God.

In the process of sexual reproduction, fertilization of the ovum (female egg) by the sperm creates what is called a zygote that divides by the process of mitosis to eventually form or produce a multicellular human being. (Ah, there's that word again, *mitosis*!) And guess what? After fertilization, the pregnancy comes to full term in about nine months. Those nine months are divided into three trimesters. Trinity! Are you beginning to notice the repetition? Our Heavenly father is so awesome. Why wouldn't the Father want His children to take after Him? For all of the confusion Satan causes, we fail to see that procreation is part of our inheritance from God.

According to the American College of Obstetricians and Gynecologists (ACOG), Dr. Draion Burch, an obstetrician and gynecologist at Magee-Women's Hospital at the University of Pittsburgh Medical Center says, "In the first month of the first trimester in the embryo the heart, lungs, brain, spinal cord and nerves, and arms and legs begin to develop. At this time the embryo is about the size of a pea! In the second month, bones appear! The genitals and inner ear begin to develop. In addition, the ankles, wrists, fingers, and eyelids begin to form. At this time the embryo is about the size of a kidney bean. After the eighth week of pregnancy and until birth occurs, a developing baby is called a fetus." Can you imagine having the development of all these functions growing inside of something so small as a kidney bean?

By the end of the second month, eight to ten of the main organs of the fetus will have formed. During the third month of pregnancy, buds for the teeth appear, and fingers and toes grow. Bones and muscles begin to grow. The intestines begin to form, and the skin is almost transparent. "I praise you Lord, because I am fearfully and wonderfully made; Your works are wonderful, I know that full well. (Psalm 139:14 NIV). The end of the first trimester (or day 1).

By the fourth month, the beginning of the second trimester, eyebrows, eyelashes, fingernails, and neck all form, and the skin has a wrinkled appearance. In addition, the legs and arms can bend, the kidneys start working and can produce urine, and the fetus can swallow and hear, according to ACOG. In the fifth month the fetus is more active. The fetus also sleeps and wakes on regular cycles. By the sixth month hair begins to grow. The Bible says, "But the very hairs of your head are all numbered. Fear not therefore, Ye are of more value than many sparrows" (Matthew 10:30–32 KJV). How can the Lord know these things if He is not present in the womb? Eyes begin to open, and the brain is rapidly developing. If the brain is rapidly developing, what information, if any, is it rapidly receiving and/or retaining? And if so, who's doing the talking? And guess what? In the midst of all of this, although the lungs are completely formed and the fetus has motion, the lungs do not yet function. If the lungs do not function, there can be no blood flow. Nevertheless, the fetus continues to grow and have movement! This is the end of the second trimester (day 2).

"In the beginning of the third trimester, the seventh month, the fetus kicks, stretches, and responds to light and sound, like music," Burch said. Eyes can open and close. During the eighth month, the fetus gains weight very quickly. Bones harden, but the skull remains soft and flexible. Different regions of the brain are forming, and the fetus is able to hiccup, according to ACOG. The ninth month is the home stretch of pregnancy, and the fetus is getting ready for birth by turning into a head-down position in the woman's pelvis. The lungs are now fully mature to prepare for functioning on their own. The new term of a full-term pregnancy is when a baby is born after thirty-nine to forty weeks. "It used to be thirty-seven weeks," Burch said.

Now, with all of this information, it still astounds me to know that according to Burch, by the sixth month the lungs are fully developed but they do not yet function, and during the ninth month the lungs are fully matured but the lungs still do not function. How is that possible? The fetus moves. His legs and arms can bend. He has fingers and toes. His intestines have begun to form. His kidneys can produce urine! He kicks, stretches, responds to light and sound, like music! And, although the lungs are completely matured and ready to function, they do not yet function. And we, the parents, other than copulation (sexual intercourse), do not have the ability to lift a finger to aide in any part of this extraordinary phenomenon of creation.

How in the world is this possible? I'll tell you how! By the Almighty God!

With God all things are possible (Matthew 19:23–30 NKJV)! God structured and prepared the product of His life system into His creation of man and woman to reproduce another human vessel as He first created it. God formed Adam out of the dust of the earth. Then God blew into Adam's nostrils the breath of life, and Adam became a living being.

Then God removed a rib from Adam and made a woman for him. I don't find it in the Bible that God blew into the nostrils of woman, but she also became a living being. I can only suppose that He did because life is not in the flesh. Life is in the blood (Leviticus 17:11 KJV). Adam said, "This is bone of my bone and flesh of my flesh." Adam did not say blood of my blood. Therefore, God incorporated man and woman to replicate the formation of flesh and bone in the reproduction of the body or creation of the man child, as we know as DNA but not the blood.

As we were taken through a description by Dr. Burch of the ACOG of how a baby forms in the womb, Dr. Burch tells us that by the sixth month, the lungs are fully developed and by the ninth month, they are fully matured but they do not yet function. The infant's lungs do not function on their own until it has been expelled from (pulled out of) the only world it has known for the last nine months and into this world of which we know as earth's atmosphere (day 3). Then, the spirit of God is breathed into the nostrils of the infant, just as He did with Adam. And the newborn takes its first independent breath. One could argue the fact that if the infant does not take the first breath of life until it is outside the womb, that life does not begin until it is born. The argument would lose its credibility because of the fact that the mother who has been given the spirit life of God from the moment she was born infuses the embryo with that same life which automatically begins to live inside the mother's womb at the moment of conception. The embryo immediately begins to live by no will of the mother, father, or of it's own. It automatically begins to grow. Where there is no life, there is no growth. The mother has no authority in the matter. The spirit life of God automatically sustains the life of the embryo, which means this event is through no will of the mother. If the mother has life, the embryo automatically has life. Remember earlier in the book when I gave the scenario of the battery in the car? Well, this would be a similar situation, but add the fact that the battery that gives life or charge to the car would also give life to a cell phone immediately after it is connected. The cell phone is not working independently. Nevertheless, the phone is connected to a life source. Once you insert your cell phone charger into the charger socket, the phone begins to charge automatically. Nothing else needs to be added. Two separate lives supported by the eternal lifeline.

When the embryo becomes attached to the life inside of its mother, it is connected automatically. The mother has no knowledge of the intricacies of how or when the embryo becomes infused or connected to the life within herself or even when that life becomes a fetus. She has no knowledge of how it breathes, how its internal organs form, or when they form. In the end (or through a procedure known as ultrasound), she just knows that they do.

And because the embryo has grown from the moment of conception, the embryo/fetus has life because it is connected to the life of its mother. Other than the fact of unfavorable conditions within the womb that would not support the fetus or the mother giving permission for someone to separate her life from the fetus (which would cause death), from the point of conception the embryo's life is automatic. A perfect example of the Almighty Father's eternal life! You only need to be connected! The spirit breath of life the mother took into her lungs as a newborn is the same breath of life that is physically and spiritually passed on to or inherited by her embryo. The breath of God is life! It is alive! It cannot die! The life in the mother will sustain the fetus until it passes into this world through the portal or matrix of his mother's womb and then receives its own first breath from God into the infant's nostrils to ignite and initiate the blood in the lungs to start him or her on the independent breathing life journey. Once that breath of God has been given by God through the mother to sustain the embryo or fetus, or the first independent spirit breath of God is gifted to the newborn, no human being has the right to take it away because no human being can give it. The embryo inherits the spirit breath of life of its mother until it becomes of age to receive its true inheritance of the breath of the spirit from the Almighty Father. God gave man the ability to create man. The ability to give life belongs to no one other than the Almighty Holy Spirit of God. But with man, because of our greed, even with all things being made possible through God, for man, it's just not enough! Man wants the impossible created by man and is constantly disappointed when it doesn't work out! However, there have been extenuating circumstances that have been forced upon women that are deemed unnecessary, a breach of privacy and even unfathomable. Upon these things I will not give opinion. These are decisions to be discussed between the person involved and God.

Life's Circle

Immediately before a child is born his world of which he is so familiar becomes disturbed. Mildly at first, but as time goes on his mild disturbance becomes annoying distractions, and the annoying distractions become massive contractions, until he has to escape. But, where does he go from here?

He has to move on. He has to find a new world. So he begins his journey. His journey is called birth.

When a child is born, its first response is to cry. He cries because he senses fear. A fear of the unknown. A fear of being taken from familiar surroundings to something new, something different. Suddenly a voice calls unto him and says, "Don't cry. I am here with you. I will take care of you." And, in time, the child comes to adjust. Because immediately after birth the child is embraced in the arms of its life's source, and slowly but surely the fear begins to lessen. The cry begins to quiet. The newborn begins to realize that it is safe.

To be safe is to be saved. Saved from the dangers that could immediately fall upon you had you not the arms of refuge to be placed into. Someone who truly loves you. Someone who will undoubtedly protect you. Someone who has anxiously awaited and prepared for your arrival.

As for us, the adult child, children of mature years have lived in the womb of the world for so long and have become so familiar with its surroundings. Then a time comes when the world of which we've become so familiar becomes disturbed, mildly at first, and as time goes on the mild disturbance becomes annoying distractions, and the annoying distractions become massive contractions, and we have to escape. But where do we go from here?

We have to move on. We have to find a new world. So we begin our journey. Our journey is called rebirth!

When a child is reborn its first response is to cry. We cry because we sense fear. Fear of the unknown. Fear of being taken away from familiar surroundings to something new, something different. Then suddenly a voice calls unto the child and says, "Fear not; for I am with you. Be not dismayed; for I am your God; I will strengthen and help you; I will uphold you with the right hand of my righteousness" (Isaiah 41:10). And in time the child comes to adjust, because immediately after rebirth the child is embraced in the arms of its life's source. The arms of refuge. The arms of someone who truly loves him. Someone who will undoubtedly protect him. Someone who has anxiously awaited and prepared for his arrival. And, slowly but surely the fear begins to lessen. The cry begins to quiet.

The reborn becomes familiar with its new surroundings.

The reborn begins to realize that he is saved. (1992)

Written by Wanda F. Kenty

CHAPTER 3
KEEPERS OF HIS FOOTSTOOL

Man and woman were given this world and everything in it. They wanted for nothing. In the beginning had they obeyed God, their children and our children would have never had to want for anything. Ever! Within the garden of Eden, God had actually created Heaven on earth! For there appears to have been a Eden in Heaven before the one on earth. Ezekiel 28:11–19 is a lamentation for the king of Tyre. Everything spoken in the lamentation was a comparison of the king of Tyre and Lucifer. Everything spoken directly concerning Lucifer was spoken in past tense.

Everything Lucifer was and had until verses 15 and 16, "Till iniquity was found in you. By the abundance of your trading you became filled with violence within, and you sinned. Therefore, I cast you as a profane thing out of the mountain of God; and I destroyed you, O covering cherub, from the midst of the fiery stones." And in Isaiah 14:12–21 (Spiritual Warfare Bible NKJV).

As we know, God created Adam and Eve and placed them in that garden, and God commanded Adam by saying, "Of every tree of the garden thou mayest freely eat, but of the tree of the knowledge of good and evil thou shalt not eat of it: for in the day thou eatest thereof thou shalt surely die" (Genesis 2:16–17 KJV). If in fact the Eden in Heaven was corrupted by Lucifer and God cast him out of the mountain of God in Heaven, then why wouldn't the kingdom which God gave Lucifer be cast out with him to become this earth? If earth is created from Heaven, God would have no need of Eden under the circumstance of which it became. It would have to be recreated to be made habitable. Ezekiel 28:16–19 supports the fact that the garden of Eden was a place of beauty and reverence that God had given to Lucifer, but Lucifer defiled his sanctuaries by the multitude of his iniquities. "By the iniquities of his trading; Therefore I God brought fire from your midst; It devoured you, and I turned you into ashes upon the earth in the sight of all who saw you." It needs to be understood that some people don't see Satan, but for those who do see him, see him for the pile of ashes of which God turned him into. This would also give reason to the two trees in the midst of the garden. God created man and placed man in the garden because in this garden was where darkness dwelt. Where darkness began! This garden was once Lucifer's in Heaven. But now Satan's garden on earth brings about a representation of two kingdoms—a kingdom of pure life and the fruit of its tree, which is the abundance of life, or the kingdom of a diluted life and the fruit of its tree of the knowledge of good and evil. Which one is to be served?

There is only one kingdom and one kingdom alone in Heaven. Unfortunately, there are two kingdoms on earth from which to choose. God and all of Heaven knew of the truth and beauty in the life in the kingdom of the Almighty God, just as they knew of the evil of Satan. God knew restoration of life and the garden of Eden on earth had to be replenished if life on earth were to continue in proper order. God created man with the light of God within him to overcome the darkness and iniquity that Satan brought with him. For this reason, God tells us how we ought to pray: Mat 6:8-13,(NKJV).

> Our Father who art in Heaven. Hallowed be thy name, thy kingdom come, thy will be done on earth as it is in heaven. Give us this day our daily bread and forgive us our debts as we forgive our debtors. And lead us not into temptation but deliver us from evil. For thine is the kingdom and the power and the glory forever. Amen.

The first command of God to man was to not eat from the tree of the knowledge of good and evil because God knew what it would do to His man. Man disobeyed. Although Adam was the person that God commanded not to eat, Eve had obviously been informed because she had the conversation with the serpent telling him what God said about not eating from the tree (Genesis 3:1–7 KJV). The serpent was the most subtle or cunning of the beasts of the field that God had made. The serpent convinced Eve that God was not being truthful with them, and she ate from the tree and gave to Adam and he also ate. Therefore, Adam, having been the one to whom God actually gave the command, was the one who had to carry the blame of disobedience. This egregious act of disobedience and distrust of God's command was the act that separated man from God. And God cursed the serpent, the woman, and Adam. So He drove out the man; God placed cherubim at the east of Eden and a flaming sword turning every way to guard the way to the tree of life (Genesis 3:14–24). Amen and Amen.

Man is this beautiful piece of workmanship that God took special time to create and also impart him with the miracle ability to procreate. He gave man the world, including all other life that God created in it, and gave him dominion over it all! Seriously, this is truly amazing! This is not some fairy tale that's read in a fictional storybook! God supplied the first man and woman with any and everything! Food, water, freedom, peace, love, happiness, trust, real estate, gold, silver, jewels, etc. With everything God had supplied, there was no need for their or our children to ever go hungry, fight with each other, or need for anything! It was the perfect setup. But no! After being given a command, man still wanted it all. He wanted what God had already given him. Plus, he wanted what God said he could not have. There was only one thing that God commanded man not to touch.

With all that God had freely given to man, there was one thing that God withheld. And man, in his disobedience, seemingly said, "No! I want that too." I suppose it could have been possible for God to have hidden the tree of the knowledge of good and evil and said nothing, but because the tree is real, as well as the sin within it, once it was found and eaten, it would then be God's fault for not telling them and putting them in harm's way. God, being the gracious God He is, does not lie nor does He change. God did not set aside the one thing that He did not want man to have just to tease him or "dangle the carrot," so to speak. God did it because He is a God of truth! He is a God of fact! He is the God of righteousness! God knew what the tree of the knowledge of good and evil consists of. God knew the reality of it. Above all, God knew the worst of it! God commanded them to protect them! But Satan knew that Adam and Eve did not know!

Because this is the earth and not Heaven, these two trees were placed in the midst of Eden's garden on earth: the tree of life and the tree of the knowledge of good and evil. The tree of life represents the life in the kingdom of Heaven. The Alpha and the Omega. There is no tree in Heaven of which one cannot eat if he needed to! The tree of life is life in its true and purest form—a piece of Heaven on earth. The tree of the knowledge of good and evil represents Satan. Two kingdoms upon this earth fighting for the lives and souls of man. One kingdom of ashes and Desolation, wants to steal, kill and destroy life, while God's kingdom wants to restore and save the lives and souls of man in Heaven, Satan was reaping the benefits of the goodness, greatness, and love of God. This allowed Satan the knowledge of God's good and greatness. Because the Almighty God is all-knowing, I don't believe that God was unaware that evil could exist, but because there was complete obedience in Heaven, there was no need for caution until Lucifer birthed evil out from himself through jealousy, envy, and covetousness. This evil is something Satan created within himself. Therefore, Lucifer could no longer reside in Heaven because it caused separation or dissension in the house of Heaven. "A house divided cannot stand" (Luke 11:17–20 KJV). Now Lucifer, while in Heaven had angels that turned away from God and also followed him. My intention is not to be too earthly in my speaking, but it is important that it is understood as exactly what I am saying. Therefore, in modern-day terms, Lucifer had become this thug-type gang leader in Heaven. Therefore, Satan was not only the most subtle and cunning of all the beasts in the field which the Lord God had made (Genesis 3:1 NKJV). He was obviously cunning in Heaven. God knows that Satan lives upon the earth and that Satan will do his duty to spread his darkness. Satan needs a following to gain power. God, our Heavenly father, never wills to hide the truth from us. He appears to be saying to man, "Trust me and obey when I give you a command or warning. It is for your own good." Through the tree of life, it was God's intent to keep the light of God's life in man to overpower Satan's darkness. But man, through his act of disobedience, gave the victory of that battle to Satan.

Now, I would like to reflect for just a moment and sort of corral all of these events before going any further just to keep a proper perspective. In the beginning God created all of this. Out of Heaven He created earth. Upon the earth, He gave light, water, the firmaments of the Heavens, the grass, the herbs that yield seed, and the fruit trees whose seed is within itself, meaning it will reproduce fruit for as long as the earth lasts. He made the stars in the sky. The sun and the moon. He created the sea and winged creatures. Every living thing that moves and creeps upon the earth. He created all the cattle and beasts of the earth. God did all of this explicitly for the comfort, support, and sustenance for the man and woman that He created. God's will was and still is for us to be His light upon this earth and to be an extension of Heaven in becoming familiar with the life and works that are done in Heaven. Adam and Eve threw it all away for a lie. And we appear to be following in their footsteps because evil is so obviously bold and unbearable in today's society! Now man wants to ask, "Where is God in all of this madness? Where is God?"

The audacity of man! Where are we for God? Seriously!

Here we are again! Back at the beginning!

In Heaven, Satan was kicked out because of his disrespect and disobedience to Almighty God. God kicked Satan and his followers out of Heaven. Now, here we are in Heaven on earth in the garden of Eden. The highest of God's earthly creation, which is man, was kicked out of the garden of Eden because they too chose to disobey God and followed Satan. As human beings, most of us know what it is to be a parent. You want the absolute best for your children. If you had the ability to create all of these perfect preparations for your children that took a lifetime for you to create and you asked them to obey one thing in return, and they chose to disobey, where would you be? God can and will not be manipulated!

I'm so glad that we are not God, because we are manipulative. However, God is still where He was from the very beginning. And even with being the disobedient, egregious, and prideful creatures we have allowed ourselves to become. God still believes in His creation. Regardless of what we have allowed ourselves to become, only God knows who we truly are. God knew that He created the earth because of Satan. God would not allow Satan to live in Heaven. And because God knows that Satan is alive in this earth, He created us to overcome Satan, not Satan to overcome us! God did not give the earth to Satan so that he could have his way. God said, "Thy kingdom come, Thy will be done on earth as it is in Heaven" (Matthew 6:10 KJV). This speaks to the fact that the life of the spirit of God is eternal. The life of Almighty God will never die! A question I have often heard at an earlier time in my life and have also asked, "If God is omniscient, omnipotent, and omnipresent He had to know what Satan was going to do. Why didn't God just kill Satan and be done with it?" The Bible says, "In the beginning was the word, and the word was *with* God, and the word *was* God. He was in the beginning with God. All things were made through Him, and without Him nothing was made that was made. In Him was life, and the life was the light of men. And the light shines in the darkness, and the darkness did not comprehend it" (John 1:1–5 NKJV Spiritual Warfare Bible). Lucifer, as well as all other Heavenly hosts and angels, were made from God, and God's life is eternal, remember? It would be the same as breaking one of the commandments. If you have broken one, you've broken them all. If God brings death to His life that lives in one of us, He would have to bring death to His life that lives in all of us.

Lucifer is not a man of flesh and blood. He was created by God in Heaven as an anointed cherub. Lucifer, at one point in his life, had the favor of the Almighty God within him, but because of his jealousy of

God, he no longer wanted the righteousness of God. Satan also knew that he could not destroy the spirit life of God within himself, so he somehow regurgitated God's spirit and willed himself to turn God's spirit inside out, from righteousness and beauty to evil and desolation, in his act of rebellion, disrespect, and rejection against the spirit life of God. But this is confirmation again that God can promise life and life more abundantly. Because God is the only one who can give life and the only one who can rightfully give permission for it to be taken away (John 10:10 NKJV). Therefore, even as Lucifer was kicked out of Heaven down to earth and earth being a part of Heaven, all are under the power of Almighty God.

"Thus says the Lord, 'Heaven is My throne and the earth is My footstool'" (Isaiah 66:1 NKJV). The Bible also says, "A house divided cannot stand" (Matthew 12:25 NKJV). The Lord did not kill Satan, but God had to put him out of Heaven. If God would kill Satan, God would have to kill us all. Who could stop evil from being replicated or guarantee that it will never happen again once it had been birthed or loosed? Therefore, the only way to remedy the situation is in battle. You are either for God, or you are against Him. If evil did not exist, what would be the need for earth? Why would there be the need of the light of God in man if there was no darkness? The kingdom of Heaven is almighty and will forever stand first. However, a new and never before prince and his kingdom attempts to rise in battle against the Almighty King of kings, and that kingdom is evil. Furthermore, I have never heard of any verse in the Holy Bible referring to a death or funeral in Heaven. God's intent was the same for His life in man to continue His light here on earth. God created man to be the light in the darkness of this world. The tree of life makes us walk as children of light. "For with thee is the fountain of life: In thy light shall we see light" (Psalm 36:9 KJV).

Many of us may feel justified by saying, "I didn't ask to come here!" And yes, that's correct. None of us did. But God predestined you to be here. And those words alone should be enough to wake you up! He created each individual for a specific reason. He knew you while you were in your mother's womb. Because of our original parents' willingness to ingest the seed of the knowledge of good and evil and because of how we have allowed ourselves to be used and confused in believing that "life is what we make it" is why that *specific reason* for which God created each one of us is not so evident in a lot of our lives right now. But let it be known, for this reason, God created us!

We are created as the keepers of the footstool of the Almighty God! Our purpose for creation is that we all were created as humans, being soldiers in the army of the Lord. We were never created to be here just to appease ourselves and do whatever we want to do. We also were not created to do whatever we can to make others' lives miserable simply because we can.

But what better ground for Satan to plant his seed than inside the father and mother of all of God's future lights upon the earth that he might infect us all and gain power over all the earth? It appears that because Satan could not succeed in taking the throne of Almighty God in Heaven, he is making a vengeful attempt to conquer His footstool.

Satan's intention was to steal the goodness of Adam and Eve and to make them rotten just like him—full of darkness. Satan knows that God equips each one of His children with personal gifts. When God created Lucifer, God gave him the gift of music. The Bible says, "Timbrels and pipes" (Ezekiel 28:13 NKJV). And those of you who don't know what your gifts are, Satan will cause distractions to prevent you from finding them. Satan desires to steal the life and disarm the weaponry God gives to His children only for the sole purpose of destroying the light and goodness within the spirit life of God. Satan also knew how powerful his evil could be, but for his evil to gain power, it had to be given life. And what better life than the lives that were created to defeat him. So, in succeeding in convincing Adam and Eve to eat of his tree, not only does Satan's evil take its first breath upon this earth. Also, Satan appears to have struck the first blow to dim the light of God's goodness by taking possession of God's greatest creation, which is man! And man sadly begins his journey into the wilderness in the footsteps of Satan as God sends them out of paradise, Heaven on earth, never to return. So he drove man out of the garden (Genesis 3:24 NKJV).

One day while listening to the Holy Spirit, I saw a vision or dream of churches of the world. I spoke to my mother about this vision. My mother, who at the age of ninety-four and of sound mind, said she had heard something like this once before. While I had not, I can only believe and accept this vision as a confirmation.

I saw as in a circus; elephants coupled together by trunk and tail while the leader walked, and the rest would follow. When the leader stopped and lifted his front legs, the ones that followed stopped and lifted their front legs and rested then on the backs of the one in front, not doing much of anything else.

The elephants represented the churches. Churches hold the greatest truth and untruth values in this world because the people of the church are the church. The knowledge of the ways of God appear to have become self-contained by the coupling of the trunk and the tail. I believe our Lord God grows weary of the same procession as do the spectators in the audience because all that are in that procession remain the same. There is so much more understanding, knowledge, and wisdom within each elephant. Each individual within the church has been given by God His own talents and gifts that He has purposed for every one of His people. The problem is we resist the uncoupling because of the fear of being different from the group. The blessing of the almighty God allows each individual to uncouple and release their individual blessings.

If you don't know what your talents and gifts are, maybe this vision may lead you to your individual questions and answers that cause you to strike up a personal conversation with the Lord to reveal in you a knowledge of which you are unaware of.

Surrender and entrust your life to God. You won't be losing anything except the sin baggage that weighs down your life. Simply talk to Him. It will only work if you believe and are expecting an answer! That is me this very moment, stepping out on faith because I have never read a book like this before. I have always been afraid to share the things the Holy Spirit has shared with me…until now!

CHAPTER 4
OUR STORY

No sooner than man gave Satan the victory of the battle in the garden, victory over the war of the future souls of this world had begun.

Now Adam knew Eve, his wife, and she conceived and bore Cain and said, "I have acquired a man from the Lord." Then she bore again, this time his brother Abel. Now Abel was a keeper of sheep, but Cain was a tiller of the ground. And in the process of time it came to pass that Cain brought an offering of the fruit of the ground to the Lord. Abel also brought of the firstborn of his flock and of their fat. And the Lord respected Abel and his offering, but did not respect Cain and his offering, and Cain was very angry and his countenance (facial expression or composure) fell. So the Lord said to Cain, "Why are you angry? Why has your countenance fallen? If you do well, will you not be accepted? And if you do not do well, sin lies at the door. And it's desire is for you, but you should rule over it." Again the Lord gave warning. Again His warning was ignored.

Now Cain talked with Abel, his brother. And it came to pass when they were in the field, that Cain rose up against Abel, his brother, and killed him. Then the Lord said to Cain, "Where is Abel, your brother?" Cain said, "I don't know. Am I my brother's keeper?" And God said, "What have you done? The voice of your brother's blood calls out to Me from the ground. Remember that the life is in the blood. So now you are cursed from the earth which has opened its mouth to receive your brother's blood from your hand. When you till the ground it will no longer yield its strength to you. A fugitive and a vagabond you shall be on this earth." Cain said to God, "My punishment is greater than I can bear! Surely you have driven me out this day from the face of the ground. I shall be hidden from your face. I shall be a fugitive and a vagabond on the earth and it will happen that anyone who finds me will kill me." And the Lord said to him, "Therefore, whoever kills Cain, vengeance shall be taken on him sevenfold." And the Lord set a mark on Cain lest anyone finding him should kill him. Then Cain went out from the presence of the Lord and dwelt in the land of Nod on the east of Eden.(Genesis 4:1–16 NKJV Spiritual Warfare Bible)

This brought about the first sin of murder upon the face of this earth in the history of mankind. Later, the family of Cain began to unfold. "And Adam knew his wife again and she bore a son and named him Seth. 'For God has appointed another son for me instead of Abel, who Cain killed.' As for Seth, to him also a son was born, and he named him Enoch. Then men began to call on the name of the Lord" (Genesis 4:25–26 NKJV Spiritual Warfare Bible).

In the Old Testament, the light of the world, which is Jesus Christ, had not yet come onto the earth. There was the Almighty God, the covenant law, the priests, and man. Being obedient to God's applications of living by the law, at least to me, seemed to be the right thing to do. On the other hand, they are hard rules to follow without eventually making a mistake. And as in the beginning of the Old Testament, many men choose not to abide by them. It has become very apparent that man does not like being told what he can and cannot do. It doesn't seem to matter to man that God's law was established for our own good. If implemented, it would save man from self-destruction. However, man appears to be telling God, "I don't like the way You are doing things. If You are God, if You are almighty, find a better way that appeals to everyone and maybe then we will accept You."

This is where our *story* begins.

Because God is Almighty and can do any and everything He wants, that very power is what entices man's greed and jealousy to increase and protect what he believes to be his own power. Possessing a power as to where no one is above you represents the maximum level of life security. Because God so fearfully and wonderfully made us, some of us have become convinced that "I'm so good, I don't need anyone else or any other help. I can survive life on my own." Man's outlook in life is as if he is saying, "I wake up in the morning. I take care of my personal hygiene. I get dressed for work. I get in my own car, and I drive to work where I make my own money. I take care of my family. God didn't do any or that! I did that! What do I need God for?"

At the end of the day you would be absolutely correct if you had completed all of that on your own, but have you ever asked yourself the question, "How did I do all of that? How did I wake up? Was it of my own will that my eyes opened?" Can you honestly say that by no other will could your eyes have remained closed? Was it by your own grace and mercy that you were able to get out of bed, take care of your personal hygiene, get dressed, get into your car, and drive to work? What about the stability of your mind and strength of your body to maintain the work you do? Can you honestly say that you possess the knowledge and power to secure that your job, and that your income stays the same or increases all by the power of your own word? And worst-case scenario, if it all falls down around you, to whom do you call out to get it back in order? Since life is power and you are life, but you did not create the power within you and you do not know where that power comes from, it should become obvious that you do not have ultimate power of yourself. So in which direction do you look for help? Upon what living power do you call? Wouldn't it seem logical to call on the one who gives life? I am not talking about our parents. They are responsible for giving us flesh and bone. But life. Life is in the blood (Leviticus 17:11 NKJV).

If you cannot believe in the living power that gave you the life you so boldly live, and you cannot prove that the power you possess is of your own free will, how can you take the credit for anything that you achieve? Whether you know it or not, that's called stealing. The family that you say you hold so dear, those children that are the world's future, if something were to happen to you and you have not taught them to believe in the power greater than themselves, what happens to them and their families? To be honest, we are seeing the effects of that this very day! Most of the things we have taught them to believe in are all lies. And as they grow older and are faced with the lies that we have forced them to believe, we create their distrust.

Take Christmas for instance. A national holiday. This one day is appointed every year to celebrate the birth of our Lord and Savior, Jesus Christ. The son of God who was sent to this earth by God to bridge the gap of the curse of the sin of Adam in the Old Testament and bring the salvation of redemption by grace from the pure blood of the sacrificial Lamb, who is Jesus Christ our Lord in the New Testament. Jesus Christ was sent as the New or the Second Adam, to restore the bond between man and God, which the first Adam destroyed. It appears that Satan is still trying to keep man separated from the one true God because, instead of celebrating our reunion with God, we go in the opposite direction and allow ourselves to get thousands of dollars in debt just to lie and blackmail our children for their profit of material gifts and label it "the Christmas spirit," instead of unwrapping or revealing to them the true and perfect gift we have been given freely from our Heavenly father.

Yes, the ones we profess to love, we blatantly lie to them and we tell them (in the name of love) that according to their behavior a jolly old man in a red-and-white suit, sporting a white beard, red hat with black belt and boots, will or will not visit to give them the things they want or maybe need. We do all we can to perpetrate a fraudulent reason to hide the true fact that we are to worship the one who was sent to this earth to redeem it from the sin of Satan so that we are no longer separated from Almighty God! But instead, we give praise to a fictitious character given the name Santa Claus or Satan Claus that supposedly "knows if you are sleeping and knows if you're awake, and knows if you've been bad or good, so be good for goodness sake." The goodness of whom? The sake of what? That is correct information of the one who sacrificed His life for us. It is perfectly good advice to teach our children of the one who Christmas truly concerns. But for what reasons we choose what we know to be a lie and go deep in debt forcing our children to believe that lie, I'll never know! Instead, we should be teaching our children the truth and embrace what we as adults and parents know as truth, as well as teaching our children to seek it. We have even come to the point where some of us have completely removed the name Christ and toppled over the cross and change the title to Merry X-mas or happy holidays, completely omitting the name Christ all together.

The same goes for the Easter bunny. Again, the nationally celebrated day for Easter is being replaced with another fictitious character. A big floppy eared bunny rabbit, that doesn't even have a name, with a basket full of stinky *unfertilized* eggs that have nothing to do with giving thanks, praise, or honor to God for the restorative resurrected life Jesus Christ had sacrificed and has given us through the grace of the Almighty Father God. (I apologize for the "stinky" eggs but a rabbit and a basket full of unfertilized eggs to commemorate the resurrection of our Lord and Savior Jesus Christ! Really!)

Easter is the celebration of the life, death, resurrection, and ascension of our Lord Jesus Christ who God sent of Himself to this world as the sacrificial lamb who was slain and His sinless blood used as atonement in exchange for the sins of our ancestors as well as the sins that you and I commit this very day. With all of the lies, the physical and mental pains and anguish that we apply upon our children and others daily, we still have the audacity to act as if we don't understand when our children hide their lives from us or don't trust us. Why should they? They know we're hiding secrets and doing things that are wrong and then punish them for doing the same. I believe children are closer to God. To hold on to the spirit of your inner child is a good thing. We are to love our children with all that is within us. We all make mistakes. You know that.

That is how Christ loves (1 Corinthians 13:4-6), because Christ knows we make mistakes.

I believe we unconsciously have memory from the womb—memory of the spirit of God imparting the product of the knowledge of goodness within our soul. Each one of us are seeds from the tree of life implanted in the soil of a womb that was created by God. But undoubtedly, after we have passed through the portal of the womb on to this earth, the longer we live upon this earth, the knowledge of evil will continue to seek us out. The spirit of this world is seeded from the tree of the knowledge of good and evil. Evil is sin and the wages of sin is death (Romans 6:23). However, each one of us has spent three days/three trimesters in the womb having the spirit of God all to ourselves placed in a physical pose the medical profession has named the fetal position, but I prefer to call it the prayer position (bowed head and bended knee). I say this because our God is an unchanging God. If in the beginning God said He was in the garden with Adam and Eve and the garden of Eden was the actual womb of life on this earth, why would God not be in the womb of life for all of His creation of man? God spoke to them of the danger that was present and to avoid it. Why wouldn't He speak to us?

In the human womb, this seed that was void and without form nine months ago has been brought to its birth's fullness of God's creation! Immediately before the new life emerges into this world, it is announced by a show of water and blood. Shortly thereafter, the birth commences. There is a separation or firmament between the womb and the newborn. After a while the separation widens creating a portal for the new life to emerge from or be pulled out of the atmosphere of purity that it shared with the life-giving God as it proceeds through the birth canal or portal, then completely expelled and enters into a world with an automatic death sentence. (Sounds familiar? Sounds like the creation of Heaven and earth to me!) In the separation of Heaven and earth, He (the Son of God) appeared as the word *light*! As a newborn child is a perfect vision of light. No darkness whatsoever! Then God said, "Let there be light!" (Genesis 1:3). For this very reason, in the beginning the light of day (Genesis 1:5) was the word. And the word became flesh (John 1:14).

To restore the separation of man from God is the reason Jesus Christ came. For this reason, Jesus Christ is called the Savior. This is why it is important to know that children replicate what they see being done, hear being said, and process the truth from the knowledge of goodness that was created in them. It isn't "not knowing" the difference between right and wrong that causes children to go astray. It is their being created with the knowledge of righteousness but watching or downloading in their mind the activity of their adult teachers and people around them doing wrong but acting as if they don't have a clue as to what has gone wrong and why their life is turned upside down, or even worse, knowing that they are doing wrong and not caring! Confusion and hidden secrets are what birth doubt and distrust in a child and adults alike. Those seeds are implanted in the soil of the womb of this earth, and at its root you will always find a lie.

I don't know what ocean or sea in Heaven the Almighty God held Satan and his followers captive, but suffice it to say, although you have read these statements a thousand times, please appease me and make it a thousand and one, but this time revealing Alpha and Omega revelations of events revealed to me by the Holy Spirit.

(Alpha) Genesis 1:1–2 says, "In the beginning God created the Heavens and the earth. The earth was without form, and void; and darkness was on (the top of the deep) the place closest to the bottom inside the water. And the spirit of God was hovering over the face the top or highest level of the waters." (I am speaking of two different sections in the same body of water.)

(Omega) Revelation 12:7–8 says, "And a war broke out in Heaven: Michael and his angels fought with the dragon; and the dragon with his angles fought, but they did not prevail, nor was a place found for them in Heaven any longer." This place not found for them in Heaven any longer was the Eden in Heaven that the book of Ezekiel 28:13 spoke about because it speaks in a past tense. Although this book of Revelation is the last book of the Bible, it is revealing an incident that has already happened. An incident that has already met its end. A place and an incident that brings about a new beginning.

(Alpha) Genesis 1:3–4 says, "Then God said, 'Let there be light'; and there was light. And God saw the light, that it was good: and God divided the light from the darkness." John 1:1–3 says, "In the beginning was the Word, and the Word was with God, and the Word was God." (The first word that God summoned was *light* Genesis 1:1–2.) John 1:2 says, "He was in the beginning with God." (He being with God implies the presence of two in the beginning, God and He.) John 8:12 says, "Then Jesus spoke to them again saying, 'I am the light of the world. He who follows me shall not walk in darkness, but have the light of life.'" And when you add the spirit of God hovering over the face of the waters equals three working bodies of one God, which is why He, God Almighty, Jehovah Elohim, the Creator, is a Trinity. The Trinity was in existence before creation began!) Genesis 1:5 says, "God called the light day, and the darkness He called night. So the evening and the morning were the first day." Therefore, on the first day of creation, God, accompanied by the spirit of God, summoned light, the first day of the world. Then God said, "Let there be a firmament in the midst of the waters, and let it divide the waters from the waters." Thus God made the firmament, by dividing the waters which *were* under the firmament, from the waters which were above the firmament (allow me to say this one last time), and (God) divided the waters (created a line of separation between the waters) which *were under the firmament* (and took them away) from the waters which were *above* the firmament, and it was so. These waters which were set above the firmament were the same "face of water" the spirit of God hovered over before God threw Satan down (Genesis 1:6–7). The same process as when God parted the Red Sea, but on a much smaller scale.

(Omega) Revelation 12:9–10, "So the great dragon was cast out, that serpent of old, called the devil and Satan who deceives the whole world; he was cast to earth, and his angels were cast out with him. Then I heard a loud voice saying in Heaven which includes all three Heavens, 'Now salvation, and strength, and the kingdom of our God, and the power of His Christ have come. Which was the Word, the light, the day of creation. For the accuser of our brethren, who accused them before our God day and night, has been cast down." The accuser is no longer in any of the Heavens. The place he has been cast down to is earth. (Alpha) And God called the firmament Heaven. His will is done in Heaven. There is no longer any form of darkness on the face of the deep. So the evening and the morning was the second day (Genesis 1:8). On the second day God created the firmament Heaven. In the beginning (the Old Testament), the only form of communication with God was between God, a holy priest, and man. When man disobeyed God and God cursed Satan, the man, the woman, and the land, there was no other way of redemption from the sins Satan passed on to man or any way for man to redeem himself for the sin he had committed against God. During this time in life, only the blood of a spotless a lamb or certain animal was acceptable for sacrifice to the Almighty God by a holy priest.

Later came a Hebrew prophet by the name of Moses who God chose to lead the Hebrew slaves out of Egypt. God showed favor upon this man and instructed him to come up into a mountain called Horeb. God talked to Moses through a burning bush and told Moses to write onto two stone tablets The Commandments, which the people of the Old Testament who followed God would live by. Later, God told Moses to build a tabernacle, which in view was a manmade structured representation of the Trinity of the Almighty God. This tabernacle was the place that man was able to come to confess his and his family's sins and offer a blood sacrifice to have his or their sins forgiven by God. God had an established procedure and order of this process of sacrifice and redemption and an order in which it was to be approached.

First, the courtyard or outside of the tabernacle which contained a cover or curtain which enclosed the tabernacle. It had only one entrance or doorway. An appointed holy priest who was ordered to be washed and cleansed and to wear special ceremonial clothes performed the actual blood sacrifices of the animals which were to be spotless and without blemish offered by the people that wanted atonement or redemption for their sins. This redemption and sacrifice were only temporary. One of the reasons being every time another sin was committed, the person had to bring another sacrifice. The holy priest acted as a mediator or official who received the animal sacrifice from that person and drained its blood on the altar to present it to God as a sacrifice offering for that person's sin. This is how forgiveness of sin was performed in the Old Testament. But this was a temporary fix because the blood of an animal, regardless of being spotless or otherwise, could not truly redeem the sinful blood of man. This again was a time in life when man lived by the laws of God (the Ten Commandments). These commandments were placed in an ark called the ark of the covenant, which were placed in an area in the farthest room from the entrance of the tabernacle called the holy of holies.

From the beginning, man could not obey the one command God made in the garden, and he hasn't made much progress since. But *Spiritual Warfare Bible (NKJV)* says an older prophet by the name of Malachi in the Old Testament, who is said to have lived about 450 years before Christ came, began to speak of a coming messenger. Christian believers today understand this messenger to be John the Baptist who would prepare the way for the true sacrificial lamb, the Lord Jesus Christ, to come to his temple. This Holy Bible also says, "And like Malachi, Christians will want to learn the lessons of God's grace in past history, while they work faithfully in the present and await God's future." Please be sure to read the entire Old Testament to get a fuller understanding of God's work with His people before the coming of His Son, Jesus Christ, our Lord.

Omega. Then came the New Testament. Revelation 12:11 says, "And they the followers of Christ overcame him Satan by the blood of the Lamb and by the word of their testimony. And they did not love their lives to the death." John 12:25 (KJV) says, "He that loveth his life shall loose it; and he that hateth his life in this life shall keep it to life eternal."

Alpha. "Then God said, 'Let the waters under the Heavens be gathered into one place, and let the dry land appear.' And it was so. And God called the dry *land* Earth, and the gathering together of the waters He called seas. And God saw that it was good" (Genesis 1:9–10).

Omega. "Therefore rejoice, O Heavens, and you who dwell in them! All of the angels and all life in all of the Heavens. Woe to the inhabitants of the earth and sea. For the devil has come down to you having great wrath, because he knows he has a short time" (Revelation 12:9–12).

Alpha. On the third day God created the earth and seas. All the rest of God's creation on earth from Genesis 1:11–31 was the remainder of God's creation until He rested.

Omega. John 1:2–5 says, "He was in the beginning with God. All things were made through Him, and without Him nothing was made that was made. In Him was life, and the life was the light of men. And the light shines in the darkness, and the darkness did not comprehend it."

John 8:12 says, "Then spake Jesus again to them saying, 'I am the light of the world earth, he that followeth me shall not walk in darkness, but shall have the light of life.'"

CHAPTER 5
LET US MAKE MAN IN OUR IMAGE

For us to understand how God created us in "their" image, we first need to have an understanding of the three persons or bodies of the Trinity—the Father, the Son, and the Holy Spirit—who they are, and what they represent.

The Father

For as long as we all can remember, there has never been a time when we did not agree upon the fact that the father of the family was considered the head or the "alpha" of the family structure. He is the source of where everything comes from for the family. The father sets the structure or foundation. The following are a few Bible verses that are used to define the Heavenly father:

> Of the Rock who begot you, you are unmindful, and have forgotten the one who fathered you. (Deuteronomy 32:18)
> God is our refuge and strength, a very present help in times of trouble. (Psalm 46:1 NKJV)
> The Lord lives! Blessed be my Rock. Let God be exalted, the Rock of my salvation! (2 Samuel 22:47)
> The name of the Lord is a strong tower. The righteous run into it and are safe. (Proverbs 18:10 NKJV)
> And he said, "The Lord is my rock and my fortress and my deliverer; the God of my strength in whom I will trust; my shield and the horn of my salvation, my stronghold and

my refuge; my savior, you save me from violence." (2 Samuel 22:2)

For who is God except the Lord? And who is a rock, except our God? (2 Samuel 22:32)

The claims of the Heavenly Father or the human father cannot be refuted, as far as His positions are concerned. However, we all are in agreement that these are the general expectations of the Father's role and character in which He is viewed upon in position within the family.

Jesus Christ, the Son of the Father

In relation to the Heavenly Father, Christ the Son is the man child of the Almighty God and the Virgin Mary (who was a descendant of King David). The son is to replicate the father, following in the father's character and way of living. The son replicating the father is the son's acknowledgment that he agrees that the ways of his father are righteous, honorable, as well as profitable, and should be exemplified. The Son desires to resemble and please the Father. At some point in His life, the Son exemplifies or replicates the role of the Father.

Jesus Christ: Almighty God Jehovah made tangible, the spoken Word, brought to light, born of flesh, and Jehovah God, so that man could see the Father, touch the Father, and know that the Father is real. "Immanuel—God with us!" (Matthew 1:23 NIV).

John 1:14, "And the word became flesh and dwelt among us and we beheld His glory, the glory as of the only begotten of the Father, full of grace and truth."

John 1:1–2, "In the beginning was the word." (Remember in Genesis 1:3, it says, "Then God said, 'Let there be light,' and there was light.") This means the very first word was God and of God! And the word that God spoke was a word of being, a noun: a person, place, or thing. God spoke or summoned that word as light, and that word became light; and the word was with God, and the word was God.

Jesus said unto him, "I am the way, the truth and the life. No one comes to the Father except through me. If you had known me you would have known my Father also; and from now on you know Him and have seen Him." Phillip said to Him, "Lord, show us the Father, and it is sufficient for us." Jesus said to him, "Have I been with you so long, and yet you have not known me, Phillip? He who has seen me has seen the Father; So, how can you say, 'Show us the Father?' Do you not believe that I am in the Father, and the Father in me? The words that I speak to you I do not speak on my own authority, but the Father who dwells in me does the works." (John 14:6–10)

And all drank the same spiritual drink. For they drank of that Spiritual Rock that followed them, and that Rock was Christ. (1 Corinthians 10:4)

Jesus Christ, the seed of God, planted in a spotless womb of God's creation of man, void of copulation, manifests the union of Heaven and earth, upon the earth. Because Mary, the mother of Jesus, was a virgin and had a love for God, afforded God undefiled, virgin ground for the spirit of God to touch down and rest upon. Because the spirit of God is life, just as the spirit of life was blown into the nostrils of Adam, who was also untouched as are the nostrils of every newborn child is virgin, If the spirit of God rests upon it or breathes into it, the gift of life is released. Just as with Mary, the virgin mother of Jesus Christ, Emmanuel, was an untouched, God filled vessel where the spirit of God touched down to rest, hovered His Holy Spirit over the womb that became the sacred soil for the seed of our Heavenly father, who brought forth the Son of God and man, from the womb of the mother of the Savior of the world.

The Father of Heaven, a female creation of God void of sin and a virgin, and the breath of the spirit of God—Trinity made holy. Just as a note: It has been said that many believe that if Jesus is the Son of God, it is impossible for God to not have had sexual relations with Mary. In man's unsuccessful effort to prove God wrong or a hypocrite, we have to think back to genesis. With God being our Heavenly Father, that, without doubt, makes Him male. Adam, who was God's first human creation and life, was also male. If a male cannot copulate with another male and form another human creation, but God can form man from the ground, make him a creation, and breathe the breath of life into Adam's nostrils, why wouldn't that same breath be just as effective being breathed onto Mary's womb? The womb was created for creation. The breath of God is to give life to His creation!

The Holy Spirit

The Holy Spirit is the third person of the body of the Trinity. He is also the hardest to describe. His actions are many, and because they are actions, they are all in the form of power. The Spirit of God is known as the bearer of life Holy Spirit. is the spirit that gives life, also known as the spirit of the Lord (mostly in Old Testament). He is known as the breath of God, the paraclete, the comforter, and the advocate, among other things. His place within the Trinity is right alongside or parallel to the Father and the Son. He is the lifeline that connects the two, so to speak. He is like the *blood* that connects and flows between the spirit vessels of the Father and the Son, like the blood that connects the functions of our bones to the functions of our flesh. "The life of the flesh is in the blood" (Leviticus 11:17).

According to Paul Gardner, editor of the book *The Complete Who's Who in the Bible,* "Both the Hebrew and the Greek words for the Holy Spirit underline the holiness of the Spirit. In the Old Testament, the adjective holy preceding the noun spirit appears infrequently (Psalm 51, 11; Isaiah 63:10–11). By contrast, the New Testament features this combination in most of its books as a frequently occurring name, especially in Acts. This does not mean that the emphasis on the Spirit is less in the Old Testament than in the New Testament. The recurring appellation for the Spirit in the Old Testament is the Spirit of God or the Spirit of the Lord; these expressions occur numerous times."

The earth was without form, and void: and darkness was on the face of the deep. And the Spirit of God was hovering over the face of the deep. (Genesis 1:2)

Now the Lord is the Spirit: and where the Spirit of the Lord is, there is liberty. (2 Corinthians 3:17)

I will put my Spirit within you and cause you to walk in My statutes, and you will keep my judgements and do them. (Ezekiel 36:27)

When He had been baptized, Jesus came up immediately from the water; and behold the Heavens were opened to Him. And He saw the Spirit of God descending like a dove and alighting upon Him. (Matthew 3:16)

By the word of the Lord the Heavens were made. And the host of them by the breath of His mouth. (Psalm 33:6)

The next day John saw Jesus coming toward him, and John said: "Behold! The Lamb of God who takes away the sins of the world!" (John 1:29–34)

This is He Jesus of whom I said, "After me comes a Man who is preferred before me, for He was before me. I did not know Him, but that He would be revealed to Israel, therefore I John came baptizing with water." And John bore witness saying, "I saw the Spirit descending coming down from Heaven like a dove and He the (Spirit) remained upon Him (Jesus). I did not know Him but He (God) who sent me to baptize with water said to me, 'Upon whom you see the Spirit descending, and remaining on Him, this is He who baptizes with the Holy Spirit.' And I have seen and testify that this is the Son of God." (John 1:30–34 NKJV)

And because of this event, God, who sent John to baptize with water, said, "This is He who baptizes with the Holy Spirit." Because Jesus, who was sent as the sacrificial Lamb of God, had become baptized with water as an action of physically washing away sin, and the spirit of God descending and remaining on Jesus was the action of the spirit of God inherently washing away sin, the promise of redemption had come upon the earth. The Father, the Son, and the spirit of God had come to earth together, in one place, at one time to consecrate Jesus Christ as the propitiation for the sins of man. The Trinity touching in agreement as one upon the earth. The wholeness of Heaven made Holy on earth.

Now that you have been introduced or enlightened to some of the images of the Trinity in their separate origins, I would like to attempt to demonstrate how their separate origins operate as one whole body and how the Holy Spirit revealed to me that we are created in their image.

Have you ever heard it said, "Your body is the Lord's temple?" Earlier in this book, you read a little about the tabernacle of meetings that God asked Moses to build for Him. My brief and extremely shallow overview of this tabernacle is by no means whatsoever to show disrespect to the description and instruction God commanded for His tabernacle of meetings. This example is only to make mention of its bodies or sections of the tabernacle, a brief description of their purposes, and how it relates to the imagery of God and how He created us in that same image.

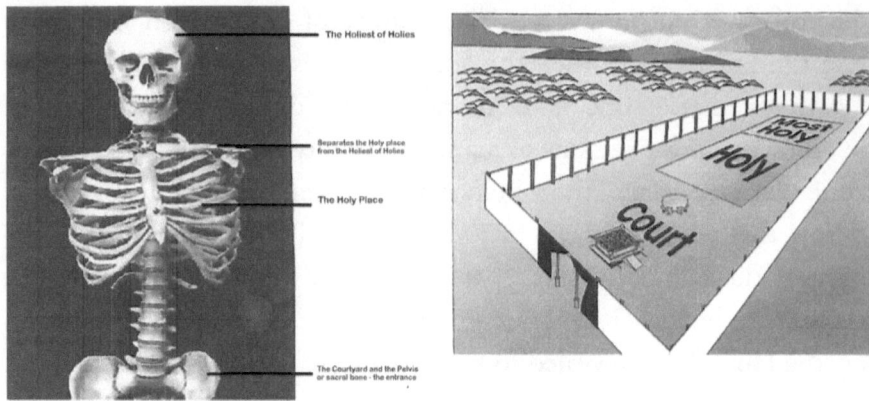

The tabernacle was meant to be a place for God to dwell among His people. It was a sacred place, a place that separated the sinful or unclean from the sinless or those made clean. It was a holding place where the holy of holies (the ark of the covenant/the Ten Commandments, Aaron's rod, and a pot of manna) were kept in the farthest east section (the innermost section) of the tabernacle. First, in the structure of the tabernacle of meetings, there was a curtain made of fine white linen that separated the outside yard from the inside or courtyard of the tabernacle. The curtain had only one entrance (which is actually the first section or portion of the tabernacle) into the courtyard, and the entrance was located on the east wall. The courtyard was where the sacrifices took place. An animal sacrifice had to be made with the shedding of blood to atone for the sin of humans that had sinned. The one to perform the blood sacrifice had to be appointed of the holy priesthood. The priests would have to go through a proper cleansing of their hands and feet standing before a bronze laver, which was a huge water basin made from the bronze mirrors of women.

This washing took place daily before they could present the blood sacrifice to God for the sinner to receive the forgiveness of God. So the holy priests were as the mediator or the holy sacrificing person, so to speak. So after entering through the gate on the east side of the tabernacle, passing the bronze laver, the sinner would approach the altar with his offering to be sacrificed, and his sacrifice was to be spotless.

(Deuteronomy 17:1). There was a process of the sinner laying his hands on the head of the animal to be sacrificed as an act of passing on his sin to the animal to be sacrificed as to release the sin from himself onto the (sinless) animal and cut the throat of the sinless animal, and the sinner was forgiven. Therefore, the animal is sacrificed instead of the man because innocent blood has to be shed for forgiveness to take place. Leviticus 17:11, "For the life of the flesh is in the blood, and I have given it to you on the altar to make atonement for your souls; For it is the blood which makes atonement for the life which it represents." (The Everyday Life Bible Amp. Version). After the blood was shed, the offering was burnt on the brazen altar by the holy priest as an offering to God, and the ashes represent God's acceptance that the sin is forgiven and could not be reclaimed.

Next was the holy place. In the Holy place there are three pieces of furniture. One piece of furniture is a golden lampstand. There were no windows in the holy place. Only the light from the golden lamp stand was used to see inside the holy place. The Bible says, "Jesus is the true light that gives light to every man." I believe that with everything that is within me. But I also believe the Holy Spirit reveals this golden lampstand as a reflection of the Trinity. I say this because the Bible also says, "Believe me when I say that I am in the Father and the Father is in me; Or at least believe on the evidence of the works themselves" (John 14:11 NIV). The golden lampstand was the only piece instructed to be made of solid gold and hammered from one piece of gold. Exodus 37:17–18 says, "Of hammered work he made the lampstand: its shaft, its branches, its bowls. Six branches came out of its sides. Three branches of the lampstand out of one side, and three branches out of the other side." The shaft of the lampstand in the center with its lamp and three branches coming out of each side for a total of seven lamps fueled by olive oil and cloth wicks. The olive oil in these lamps are to never burn out. Its ornamental knobs and its flowers were of the same piece. The Almighty Father God stands as the all in all of the tree of life as the center shaft and the other two of the Trinity on either side of Him working as one instrument. The Son of God, Jesus Christ, the cloth that burns and contains the light of the world that is to never go out, fueled by the oil of the Holy Spirit. The seven bowls that stem from and are connected to the shaft, hold the oil that ignites the flame and life of the Holy Spirit. The heartbeat, the constant pounding of eternal life.

Then there was the table of bread.

> The Lord said, "And you shall take fine flower and make twelve cakes with it. Two-tenths of an ephah shall be in each cake. You shall set them in two rows, six in each row, on the pure gold table before the Lord. And you should put pure frankincense on each row that it may be on the bread for a memorial, an offering made by fire to the Lord. Every Sabbath he shall set it before the Lord continually, being taken from the children of Israel by an everlasting covenant. And it shall be for Aaron and his sons that they shall eat it in a holy place; for it is most holy to him from the offerings of the Lord made by fire, by a perpetual statute." (Leviticus 24:5–9)

Then there was the altar of incense. Exodus 30:6–8 (NKJV), "And you shall put it before the veil that is before the ark of the testimony, before the mercy seat that is over the testimony where I will meet you. Aaron shall burn on it sweet incense every morning when he tends the lamps, he shall burn incense in it. And when Aaron lights the lamps at twilight, he shall burn incense on it, perpetual incense before the Lord throughout our generations." This sweet fragrance is as the open and honest conversation of prayer and supplication unto the Lord. As we assume the prayer position, on our knees, prostrate, or even what I believe to be the original position of prayer, the fetal position, bowed head and bended knees, our bodies take the position of the tabernacle. With our face to the ground, the spine of the tabernacle with its sockets and boards coupled together at the top and bottom by one ring, and he made the middle bar to pass through the boards from one end to the other.

There was a veil: the door to the holy of holies. The veil was hung horizontally from four bars of acacia wood that separated the holy from the most holy room of the tabernacle.

The innermost room was called the Holy of Holies or most holy, where God dwells. It was covered by a veil, and no one was allowed to enter except Israel's high priest. That happened only once a year on Yom Kippur (the Day of Atonement) to offer blood of sacrifice and incense before the mercy seat.

In comparison to the tabernacle that was manmade to honor God, we will take a look at the human vessel God made "in His image" for man.

The Skeleton

As I spoke earlier about the lies we feed our children about holidays and their meaning, another pagan holiday or festival that we acknowledge is Halloween. One of the main props of this pagan festival is a skeleton or the skull of a skeleton. Skeletons have been associated with the dead for a long time, but in all actuality, Satan's modus operandi is to always operate in the exact opposite of God. "Satan wants to turn you away from your innermost being by making it appear to be a foul or scary thing, But on the contrary, that is our body's Holy of Holies. No one is allowed inside," but God! In fact, the skeleton is very much associated with life while the blood is still present in the body.

According to the *Human Anatomy and Physiology Laboratory Manual Cat Version,* fourth edition By Elaine N. Marieb, RN, PhD, at Holyoke Community College, "The skeleton is constructed of two of the most supportive tissue found in the human body—cartilage and bone. Besides supporting and protecting the body as the internal framework, the skeleton also provides a system of levers with which the skeletal muscles work to move the body. In addition, the bones store such substances as lipids and many minerals (most importantly calcium). Finally (and most importantly to life), the red marrow cavities of the bone provide a site for hematopoiesis (blood cell formation)." Leviticus 17:11 (NKJV) says, "Life of the flesh is in the blood," meaning this is where our cells for blood are formed. The skeleton is our storehouse of life.

Also, according to Elaine Marieb, RN, PhD, in the section "Chemical Composition of Bone," "Bone is one of the hardest materials in the body. Although, relatively light, the bone has a remarkable ability to resist tension and shear force that continually act on it. An engineer would tell you that a cylinder like a long bone is one of the strongest of its mass. Thus, nature has given us an extremely strong, exceptionally simple almost crude—a natural or raw state, not yet processed or refined, and flexible supporting system without sacrificing mobility. The skeletal system is the foundation of the human body. The body is as the building, and the skeleton is as the foundation of which the materials of that building rests upon.

The main structures I would like to bring into focus are the five structures that form the tabernacle or vessel of man. These are the sacrum, the bony thorax or rib cage, the clavicle, the spine, and the skull.

In this synopsis, I will attempt to give a visual aide of how we are physically created in the image of God's Trinity as a sacred vessel, as they are individually sacred—the blueprint of how we were created by the hands of God so that the Trinity would always be with us individually and the reflection of how God used man and woman to create a sacred tabernacle with our hands for God to be with us and have a relationship with Him upon this earth before the coming of His Son. Man was God's first tabernacle. Because the Christ had not yet come, like in the beginning, God brought the Trinity to earth to dwell with man. Before I continue I must say, as I stated in the beginning of this book, I prayed to the Father that His Holy Spirit would lay foundation for this message presented. I prayed, and will repeat, may I not speak anything that is not of His will. I pray these words to follow are not for self-gratification but for the glorification of our Almighty God who is worthy to be praised. God's instruction to Moses was to make the tabernacle as one piece, as one body. In comparison to the illustration of the tabernacle of meetings and the vessel of man in the skeletal illustration, what do you see?

First is the sacrum. This is the only gate or entrance to God's truth of creation or tabernacle of man. The place where human genesis of the flesh takes place. "God said, 'Let us make man in our own image, after our likeness: and let them have dominion over the fish of the sea and the fowl of the air, and over the cattle, and over every creeping thing that creepeth upon the earth.' So God created man in His own image, in the image of God created He him: male and female created He them" (Genesis 1:26–27). After God blessed the man and the woman, He blessed them with a portion of their inheritance of the ability to create flesh and bone from the Almighty God of which they were created.

(Refer to the skeleton and tabernacle.)

"Jesus said unto him, 'I am the way, the truth and the life. No man come to the Father except through me'" (John 14:6 KJV). The sacrum is also known by many around the world as "the sacral or holy bone." I have taken a partial paragraph from *The Mesoamerican Sacrum Bone: Doorway to the Otherworld* by Brian Stross.

Allow me to first say I am not a follower of the Mesoamerican beliefs. As a matter of fact, this is the first time I have read about it. However, in my research for information concerning this bone, it does explain an interesting and most informative view of how and why the name for this bone came about. Because we were originated from the will of our God in Heaven and were brought to fruition by way of our human father's seed and the life connection within our mother's womb, the sacral region holds the soil for the root of the fruit of man and through natural birth or by cesarean or C-section. The region of this portal is the only way by which we can enter this world. I have also included the entire abstract from which I obtained this information so that you may further research it yourself. However, I am in no way trying to insert this information as a gospel truth.

This paragraph portion states, "While most bone names readily reveal their origins, it has long been a mystery why the sacrum bone *os sacrum* should be called the 'holy bone.' That it is a translation from the Greek *hieron osteon* merely pushed the inquiry back from the first Latin use in about AD 400 to the time of Hippocrates (about 400 BC). The sacral region is the only way flesh can enter this world. Because Adam and Eve gave way to sin, we as the offspring are naturally born into the sin they committed. The gate of the sacrum is the only door or portal by which man can be replicated. In the tabernacle, the gateway or doorway is attached to a curtain that completely surrounds the inside of the tabernacle just as our own flesh completely surrounds the insides of our human tabernacle or vessel. That curtain, like our flesh, is the outward representation of the life of which it contains. In the tabernacle of meetings, this curtain surrounds and contains all of what the Father God regards as the holiness of Himself. That's why the tabernacle was a holy tabernacle. The Father God is holy and without sin. Just as our curtain or flesh is a representation of the life that is within us because God created us, man and woman. Adam and Eve, were created holy but opened the door to the thief that seeks to steal, kill, and destroy us from the ability of being restored and returned to our maker. But thank Almighty God for bringing Himself out from the invisible to the visible. Thank Almighty God for using the flesh of the woman to surround Himself that He would enter this world and reclaim His creation. The Father, the Word, became flesh, the visible curtain or covering that surrounds and contains all of what the Father God regards as the holiness of Himself. Jesus Christ, the spotless Lamb, the Savior and Redeemer of the lost. The entire surrounding of the tabernacle is a curtain which represents the skin or boundaries of the individual tabernacle as a whole. If you do not enter through this one entrance of the tabernacle of meeting, you remain with your sin. Christ Jesus is the body of the tabernacle of God. The only way to come back to God is through the gateway or door of Jesus Christ. Once you enter in, you are accepted to be freed from your sins, no matter what they are. Only blood can atone the sin of man (Leviticus 1:4 NIV). And today, because Jesus Christ has come, He is the sacrificial lamb for all the sins of this world that man has committed. He lives in the courtyard within us and willingly sheds His blood for our sins if we would just ask and believe. That is why He is referred to as the Sacrificial Lamb of God.

Moving deeper into our God-created vessel is the rib cage. It forms a protective cone-shaped cage around the vital organs that are housed in the thoracic cavity. For example, the heart and lungs, the stomach, kidneys, and it partially covers the liver. These are all vital organs that deal with the moving and cleaning of blood within our bodies. "For the life of the flesh is in the blood" (Leviticus 17:11). The bony thorax is located in the middle of the body. It holds the same location as the holy place in the tabernacle.

And in God's vessel of the man, the human heart and lungs as one component, represents the golden lampstand. It is located in the body in the same area as the golden lampstand. Within the human heart, also composed of its many intricacies are its primary structures that include the aorta, which is situated atop and center of the heart. (The shaft of the golden lampstand.) The right and left atria, the right and left ventricles, and the pulmonary and systemic circuits. It also comes fully equipped with its own electrical or lighting system that is to never go out. The heart and the lungs, like the lampstand, are of one whole piece. The heart's purpose is to remove from the blood, by way of the lungs, blood that has become unclean and make it clean again (Jesus Christ) to make it whole and usable to daily sustain the entire body. One solid unit and all of its intricacies, hammered or pounded, formed into one unit. The heart is continually pounding via electrical impulses. The light of life!

Like the holy priest, Jesus Christ removes the unclean life in the body and carries it back to the spirit breath of God that was blown into the nostrils of man to receive God's eternal cleansing breath, but man has to choose to keep it. The heart's main function is to continually cleanse the blood and sustain the light of life within it. That is why it is our duty as the priests of our temple to attend to ourselves in the manner of which God so ordered, that our physical, as well as our spiritual, light does not falter. Our conscious heart, the table of incense, are our prayers that we send up in word to the Lord God as a sweet fragrance to Him of His word in and over our lives as well as the communion we take with Him in bread as a symbol for the body as well as bread of the Word of God to sustain the spirit. Also, the wine represents the pure blood that atoned the sin of man. "Then Jesus was led up by the Spirit into the wilderness to be tempted by the devil. And when He had fasted forty days and forty nights, afterwards He was hungry. Now the temper knowing of Jesus' hunger came to Him and said, 'If You are the Son of God, command these stones to become bread.' But He answered and said, 'It is written, "Man cannot live by bread alone, but by every word that proceeds from the mouth of God"' (Matthew 4:1–4 NKJV).

The Holy of Holies: the veil in our temple that separates the Godhead from the rest of the body of man. The clavicle or collar bone (its origin from the Latin *clavicula*, meaning "little key, tendril, door-bolt") is also the only long bone in the body that lays horizontally. It lies at the top of the rib cage between the neck and skull or head and can be easily seen in the frontal view of a thin person.

God created man in their image. Man was not created to create his own image. God created man to have life and to have it more abundantly. In the beginning, the tree of life was our covenant. There was no need for an ark because Almighty God is the head of man. His throne is always on top because no one can ascend the Lord that they could ever look down on Him. But when man chose to disobey God, the sin of man was what separated us from God (Isaiah 59:2 NKJV). Therefore, without God as the head, our bodies become useless to Him because there is no order or facility from which to receive the correct information. The Holy of Holies held all that was sacred to the actions and beliefs in our lives: the Ten Commandments, the letter that we were to uphold the way and word of our Lord, the rod of Aaron, one of the twelve rods. The Lord God ordered Moses to bring before the tabernacle of meeting the rod of the house of Levi. "And it shall be that rod of the man whom I choose will blossom; thus I will rid myself of the complaints of the children of Israel, which they make against you" (Numbers 17:4–5 NKJV).

Also, a jar of manna that God instructed Moses who delegated it to Aaron. These commandments, trusts, and beliefs are what God has given us as a guide to how He expects us to live our lives. This area in the creation of man is where the spoken word of God is heard and comprehended. This is the area of which our senses live: the eye to see, the ear to hear, the tongue to taste and talk, the nose to smell, and the nerve endings in our skin that allow us to receive touch through the receptors of a miraculous brain that God created in us to keep us in contact with Him.

Remember, immediately after you came to being in your mother's womb, in the very first month of your first trimester, within the first four weeks of your making, God began to develop your heart and lungs (the holy place, the golden lampstand that is never intended to go out), the brain, spinal cord, and nerves (the Holy of Holies, the ark of the covenant), even your arms and legs, and you were just the size of a pea! Just like the tablets of commandments, the rod of Aaron, and the jar of manna that God placed in the ark of the holy of holies, I believe God has placed something or some things specific in each one of our holy of holies, and it is for each one of us to ask of Him and to search it or them out. "More than anything that you guard and protect your mind, for life flows from it" (Proverbs 4:23 CEB). That is the mission I am attempting this very moment.

A Reflection of the Trinity

Almighty God, Jesus Christ, and Holy Spirit,
You said, "In your image you made me to be."
But, as I gaze at my image I'm standing alone,
Though in you stands an image of three.

The Almighty God, the *rock* of my salvation,
Who surrendered His Son to the tree.
In omnipresence, your Trinity paid this incredible
Price, just for me!

Born of a virgin, the Word became *flesh*,
Christ Jesus, the Redeemer of sin.
Omniscient of all sin, in His flesh, like a blanket.
Spread His Word as my cover of skin.

Between my flesh and my bone lays a spirit sublime.
Most Holy omnipotence reign.
Laid atonement for all sins on Calvary's hill
With innocent *blood* from the Lamb that was slain.

Thank You, Jesus!

Now, the gaze of my image is so much more than myself.
I know now that I am never alone.
Christ Jesus my *flesh*, the Holy Spirit my *blood*, and

Almighty God Jehovah, my *bone*. (May 18, 1993. Revised, July 22, 2018. Revised August 21, 2018. Revised October 24, 2018)

Written by Wanda F. Kenty

CHAPTER 6
WE ALL ARE THE CHILDREN OF THE ALMIGHTY GOD

The Lord God has blessed me with talents and gifts of the Spirit. Among those are spirits of happiness and love. Talents that I have been given that make me happy are dancing and singing, as well as the gift of the pen. But, what good are these gifts and talents if I keep them to myself? Satan had me bound for a very long time. I knew I had these gifts and talents, but at that the same time I didn't know that's what they were. I saw them as hobbies, things I liked to do, but I didn't see them as tools that I could use in helping someone else. Very rarely would I do them in public because I didn't want to appear as a show-off or an attention-seeker. So I stuck to the one thing I knew I could do and had great confidence in doing, which was being of service to other people. Whether it be haircare, childcare, home healthcare, elderly care, it really didn't matter. I convinced myself that I was doing good deeds for people that needed it, and it kept me making an honest living. But truth be told, after working two jobs for thirty-three years, I found out that I really had been a good servant because people were usually pleased with my services. So much so, they would never want me to quit. But I began to realize that I had lost the happiness inside myself.

I had been serving so many others that I had no room to serve or give attention to myself. I began to realize I didn't know who I was. I especially did not know who I was to God. I knew who and what I meant to other people and what I was doing to make a living. But, what am I doing to make myself happy and know why and what God created me to be for Him? I knew that what I had been doing were good things to do, but was that all? It wasn't until this second trimester of my life (because God said that He would give man 120 years Genesis 6:3 NKJV), that I began to realize that the only time I felt real joy and solace was when I was singing or writing. While in praise and worship service, I found myself singing louder than the whole congregation. I knew in my heart that I wasn't trying to show off and that little voice outside of me kept telling me to lower my voice, but I couldn't because in my soul, I was truly happy. Then I began to wonder, "How many other people in this room that can hear my voice want to do the same thing but have also felt embarrassed to do so?" I am not attempting to make my voice a focal point but mainly proclaim the name of our Creator and have no shame, whatsoever! Even if I mess up! I really don't care! The fact that I am no longer afraid to sing out loud, especially in praise, just might encourage another person to let their light of what they love shine also. The Bible says, "Neither do men light a candle, and put it under a bushel, but on a candlestick; and it giveth light to all that are in the house. Let your light so shine before men, that they may see your good works, and glorify your Father which is in Heaven" (Matthew 5:15–16). And these good works are not the sound of my voice but the happiness that resonates from the joy of lifting up the name of the Lord! So for all these years, I found I had been hiding one of the lights He had given me for fear of what others might say. This puts me in the mind of a writing of one that I believe to be a truly powerful writer by the name Marianne Williamson who wrote, and I quote:

> Our deepest fear is not that we are inadequate.
> Our deepest fear is that we are powerful,
> Beyond measure.
> It is our light, not our darkness that most frightens us. Your playing small does not serve the world.
> There is nothing enlightened about shrinking
> So that other people won't feel insecure around you. We are all meant to shine, as children do!

It is not just in some of us; It is in everyone!
As we let our own light shine, we unconsciously give
other people permission to do the same.
As we are liberated from our fears,
Our presence automatically liberates others.

These are words of wisdom that truly speak to my heart and words that each one of us need to memorize and incorporate in the souls of our mind and echo throughout our lives. You will more than likely find that what you fear most just may turn out to be one of your most powerful weapons that God has given you because that is the weapon Satan is so diligently trying to prevent you from using or developing. So for those of you who do believe there is a God, I hope this book will help you to come to know who, what, how, why, and where He is in Heaven and in you. For those of you who do not believe there is a supreme being, those that do not believe that the Almighty God exists like it or not, you are one of Satan's greatest weapons because, as long as you don't believe in God, Satan has full reign over you because there is nothing or no one else to believe in, especially yourself. It seems that the atheist compares the choice of Almighty God and Satan as if going to the voting polls. If they don't like either of the two choices running for office, they choose to not vote for either one and move on to another issue.

It appears to me that they are under the impression that they will just have to accept what happens! Well, that's close but you can't come out of this voting booth without a choice. If you don't choose God, the lever automatically is pulled for Satan. Heaven is an atmosphere of life and, there is only one way Heaven offers it and that is to have it and have it more abundantly through knowing the Father who is in Heaven and through Jesus Christ. Earth being created from Heaven is also an atmosphere of life but, we have accepted or chosen two ways to live it: On earth as it is in Heaven or, by the knowledge of good *and evil!* It's impossible for you to live your own life because you did not create your own life. I believe the best you can do in that case is guess your path for your own life but, you will have to suffer your own consequences.

If you do not surrender your life back to the one who created you, you automatically keep the seed you inherited from the one who despises your Creator. Satan, for a fact, knows all too well that God does exist, and he is equally if not more satisfied with the fact that you don't care to know. Satan is totally happy with receiving the residual. Every human life God created is so much more than the lie Satan wants so desperately for you to believe.

On September 18, 2018, my new home church, Rhema Christian Center, under Apostle, now Bishop, LaFayette Scales, located at 2100 Agler Road in Columbus, Ohio, held an event where many of the churches in Columbus came together for an evening of praise and worship. The event was entitled "One Night." I remember arriving early as Apostle reminded us in church service that a full house was expected. Attendance met his expectation as the church was filled to capacity and resulted as one of the most enlightened services I have ever had the pleasure of attending. The presence of the Lord was so heavy and full as the praise lifted ever so high and weightless.

I remember after being led to my row I was seated alone. Shortly thereafter, a very young man was led to my same row. We sat separated at first then were asked to not slack the seating as to make room for those remaining. As we came together, we began to introduce ourselves and became engaged in conversation about our home churches. The young man introduced himself as Niko. While in conversation, Niko informed me that he used to be an atheist. Of course at that point I was totally intrigued with what he had to say as he ended up in a meeting of praise and worship. He said at one point in his life he did not believe in God. He began to tell a story of how he made his friend a bet. He said if his friend would give him so many weeks (I don't want to misquote the exact number), he (Niko) could prove to his friend that God did not exist. Niko went on to say that in the gathering all of the information in his defense that there was no God was the very information that revealed to him that God truly did exist. He said, "In my mission to disprove there was a God, I became a believer and I will forever believe!"

And I said hallelujah with a big smile. And as one of the sayings of our church to new believers, I said to him, "Welcome home!"

I asked Niko for permission to enter our conversation in this book, and he gladly said yes and offered to personally write his last name because I did not want to misspell it. His last name is "Troche." Just hearing his testimony was like the icing on the cake, for nothing else could have topped my elation of that praise and worship event! Before the night was through, two more young men came and joined the circle of prayer that the congregation was asked to form. The two young men that joined us were in their late teens as was Niko. These three young men were very powerful in prayer as they patiently awaited the Holy Spirit to come. It was just the four of us in our prayer circle. These three young men in their late teens and myself being sixty-one years young at the time gave me the impression that God was infusing past and future revelation into present praise. I said that I would claim that day as a new day and time with my personal Shadrach, Meshach, and Abed-"Niko!" That was a night I will always remember! God's Word is still at work. And if you are an atheist or haven't decided that God is real, reconsider what you have read in this book. Come to know who you are in Christ and exactly who Jesus Christ is in you and all of what the Father did to create us in their image.

Don't simply choose not to believe in God. Begin to read His Word and try to find where His Word comes back void.

God created man in His image so that man could continue to create man in their image. God never created Adam and then said to him, "After I created you, whatever you and the Misses can create or come up with is up to you!" No! Every human vessel that God created from the creation of man until this very day was and still is created in their image. If nothing else, take this thought into consideration. I know it may seem a little far-fetched, but not so much so if you truly consider what is being said.

We all know, whether we believe it or not, that when we speak of the Trinity we are speaking of a body of three: the Father, the Son, and the Holy Spirit. In the tabernacle of meetings, the Bible says the place where God the Father dwelt was in the innermost or deepest portion of the body of the tabernacle, the Holy of Holies. "Of the Rock who begot you, you are unmindful, and have forgotten the one who fathered you" (Deuteronomy 32:18 NKJV). In the center of the tabernacle, the Holy Spirit of the light and bread of life was in the holy place, the place of moving and restoration. "The earth was without form, and void: and darkness was on the face of the deep. And the spirit of God was hovering moving over the face of the deep" (Genesis 1:2 NKJV). Jesus Christ as the gate of the tabernacle: "Jesus said unto him, 'I am the way, the truth, and the life. No one comes through the Father except through me'" (John 4:16 NKJV). Therefore, in the interest of these three separate expressions of the Trinity, I ask you to consider this expression of how we were made in the image of their Trinity: a three-part being, being one God.

Because our physical bodies are compartmentalized as flesh, blood, and bone, each compartment contains individually what you are made of, but not the total sum of what you are. Your bones or skeleton by themselves would make up the framework of the body, but that would not be the sum of you. You would have stability and the ability to bear weight, but there would be no weight to bear. Your flesh is an excellent cover and protection, but (by itself, without the blood and bone) it has nothing that needs protecting. And your blood, because it is the storehouse of life, is extremely valuable, but it lacks anything that it can bring to life (without flesh and bone).

Now, keep in mind that all of these are the sum of who you are. Separated, all three have a purpose, but being separated from each other, they simply cannot serve a total purpose. But if we establish the framework or the skeleton and then apply the flesh, combining the two, we have one body, house, or vessel with the ability to function when blood supplies the life. That is exactly what God did when He created man. He created the bone and flesh out of the earth. However, it had no life until God blew the spirit of the life of God into the nostrils of man, then man became one living being. Three parts, one being. This is exactly how we were created in their image. The Lord God is like our framework, our rock, and our strong tower. The evidence of a life-bearing vessel that is virtually impossible to destroy! The Lord and Savior Jesus Christ. The Word which became flesh is our redeemer. Man was created in the image of God from the earth that was created from Heaven. The Holy Spirit, the breath of life from the mouth of the Heavenly Father, is how we are created from the Trinity of the Father, the Son, and the Holy Spirit generated from the Heaven that started it all. One created vessel that represents the three Godheads. One God who is the three Godheads. No one can get to the Father, our framework, the innermost of the body, unless they come through the flesh, the Word, Jesus Christ, who became flesh, the outermost body. And the life of the blood that constantly beats between the two.

I stress this fact because the Bible talks about an incident that I would encourage you to read, which is Luke 16:19–31. It speaks about a rich man and a poor man named Lazarus. The rich man, while alive, was not sympathetic to the poor. When they asked for his help he would not help, but the rich man had more than enough to spare. It came to pass that they both died. The rich man was sent to Hades and was tormented. The poor man was taken up by angels to Abraham's bosom. Now the tables were turned and the rich man needed help from Lazarus and called out to Abraham, but Abraham could not help him because there was a chasm, a separation that neither side could cross. The rich man said, "Well, if you can't save me, I have five brothers. Go warn them so they don't end up here!" Abraham said, "Let them listen to Moses and the prophets. If they will not listen to them, they will not listen to me."

You see, there is still time while you have life in your body to search the truth, because when life is called to leave the body, death comes to the flesh. That flesh is the same vessel God created before He blew the breath of life into your nostrils. It is the same vessel you will mourn that lays in the casket at a funeral. But that spirit life goes to its place of which God determines. And once determined by God, there's no turning back. Therefore, as God is good and evil is bad, and evil is upon this earth right now, you don't have to die in sin with no chance of ever knowing true life and the beauty of eternal life in Heaven after life on earth. If you don't ask for forgiveness and ask the Lord Jesus Christ to come into your life, you and your loved ones will either be reunited in Hades or hell in torment, reunited in Heaven in true life everlasting, or if one goes to one place and the other does not, then you never see each other again.

So please, for the sake of true life, make a sacrifice and search until you find the one that holds the truth and in which one you will find the lie. That is my purpose for this book. I want you and I to get to the true side: Heaven!I want to see all of everyone I already know and meet new friends. I want you to be there too. But if you don't learn the life of God on earth, there will be no use for you in Heaven. What you know how to do here on earth that is pleasing to God, and is done in the name of God, is the basis of what God will use you for in Heaven. So if you would please start seeking God's Word. But first, know these basic things about our Creator and how He relates to us:

In the beginning, there was God, the spirit of God, and the Word of God.

"Let there be light!"

God pulled earth out of Heaven.

God set the firmament of the Heavens between the Heaven and earth.

This separation between the waters that were in Heaven from the waters of darkness that was upon the face of the deep had later been somewhat replicated here on earth, but on a much smaller scale, when God made a firmament or space through the Red Sea to separate His people from their enemy. The separation in Heaven was far greater because Heaven is eternal. The enemy was taken away from Heaven forever because there is no darkness in Heaven. Life here on earth is but for a time. Nevertheless, the Almighty God placed a firmament or space in the waters between His people to escape the enemy of darkness that pursued them upon this earth.

God prepared the earth to make it habitable for life with food and water.

God pulled man out of earth.

God pulled out of Himself "the breath of life" and blew His life into the nostrils of man that man would be given the breath of life.

God pulled woman out of man. God made the man child to be pulled out of woman, it is (just now) being revealed to me that if God pulled earth out of Heaven, then Heaven would also be male or masculine because the earth is the womb or matrix for all creation, like the woman is the womb for both creations of human vessels. Because child was pulled out of the first woman, the first woman was pulled out of the first man. The first man pulled out of or created from the earth and the earth was pulled out of Heaven.

Life on earth for man would then commence. If we would simply stop and reflect on that thought for a moment. There is no evil in any and all that God created. God has not added or taken away anything from His beginning of creation to this very gift of today. So, what happened? What changed things?

It was the ingestion of the fruit from the tree of the knowledge of good and evil and the willing disobedience of man. But always remember, "For God so loved the world, that He gave His only begotten son, so that whoever believes in Him should not perish but have eternal life" (John 3:16 NKJV).

When Jesus Christ was on calvary surrendering His life in exchange for our salvation, He surrendered the whole armor of God from Himself and extended to all that might receive it in continuing His gospel of peace.

Peace by Piece

Jesus took off His whole armor,
He surrendered it all willingly.
He removed every piece from His head to His toe,
And extended it all toward me!
He removed His helmet of salvation.
He placed it upon my head,
to reveal His face, to renew my mind,
and wore my crown of thorn instead.
He took off His breastplate of righteousness
as sin came to ravage His flesh,
Tearing in pieces, down to His bone,
and gently placed it upon my chest.
He took off His shoes, laced them onto *my* feet,
for my journey in His gospel of peace.
Through *His* was driven a nail, in attempt to unveil
His weakness,
yet His love never ceased.
His shield and His sword he placed into my hands
releasing faith and God's word without loss.
Surrendering all defense as He opened His hands,
then they too were nailed down to the cross.
Sin thought it had won mistaking ignorance as fun,
casting lots as they parted His raiment.
But I part truth unto you; they know not what they do,
as His forgiveness is price, in *full payment.*
So I rejoice in the resurrected body from the cross,
for His death brought salvation to me.
I will forever put on the whole armor of God,
because Jesus Christ took it all off *for* me. (May 27, 2012.
Revised May 28, 2012. Revised July 22, 2018)

Written by Wanda F. Kenty

In our world, the evil of that one little seed has taken root and spread like wildfire. It has become a truly horrid and twisted tree. As hard as it tries to rise, his trunk has never left the ground, for it was cursed to be on its belly and eat dust all the days of its life. Its branches hold no perch for the fowl of the air, nor can its leaves provide shelter from the sun. His sticky black sap lurks and tries its best to devour all that comes upon its path. In this substitute version of life that Satan has produced, we have become further enticed by negative forms of music, television, and social media where every idea and lifestyle demands to be respected, when most of its ideas and lifestyles are the farthest from respectable.

In 1967, a secular vocal group who called themselves the Fantastic Four had a hit record titled "The Whole World Is a Stage." (And everybody's playing a part.) However, I do believe it was the world renown playwright and poet William Shakespeare who was first to coin the phrase. Nevertheless, no other statement could have been closer to the truth. The title of that song and phrase is *our story.* The characters we play on the stage of this world are not the true individuals we were created to be. Deep down inside, each one of us would rather be known or remembered as someone that achieved or lived a great or phenomenal life. We all want to appear fearless. That is why the platform of the stage of this world is so readily embraced. However, the premier of this world was written and produced by the Almighty God, our true and natural Father. The true and natural introduction of this world was a beautiful garden that was in Heaven, full of righteousness, beauty, riches, truth, and love. It was created to support the true intention for Holy family life: 1) the Almighty Heavenly Father, 2) the man child that was pulled out of the dust of the earth and created by the hand of the Almighty Father, and 3) the woman that was pulled out of the man God had created as man's help meet. Therefore, in the beginning of human life, we have the Heavenly Father God, the first son, Adam, and the first daughter, Eve. That is the true making of every family on the face of this earth. The Heavenly Father, the Son (to become a father), and the daughter (to become mother). Because of our Heavenly Father who made us in their image, it is the father or man child that determines every future male and female on the face of this earth. In the garden of Eden in Heaven, and in all of Heaven, there is only one throne. Upon this earth, where Satan was cast down, in the center of the garden of Eden are a representation of two thrones: the tree of life, which makes the statement on this earth that God said, "Heaven is My throne and the earth is my footstool." And even though the footstool is far smaller than the throne, make no mistake, it is still held as part of a set and it is still God's property!

Within the tree of life, we are to have the life that God intended and to have that life more abundantly. Within the tree of the knowledge of good and evil, we were given a choice of playing the good, being good like God, because goodness has already been established in God's man. Or we feed off of the ingested ability that enables man to change and become selfish by playing the role of the villain by making or becoming our own god, which would turn us away from the worship of the goodness of our exalted God as we would eventually become evil in the likeness of Satan. The mixed seed Adam and Eve chose to ingest allowed confusion to interfere with our obedience to God because they had taken into themselves the knowledge of something other than goodness that Adam and Eve never knew existed until they disobeyed and ate of it. That seed became a part of their DNA. That mixture has now been passed down to all of us. The moment that happened, we all were given the opportunity of choice.

To choose God was never an option that God gave to Adam because God had already chosen him! For God to be chosen by Adam was never a gift from God. And because of this, we have all become actors in a useless attempt to convince each other in believing that we are in control of our lives when all the while we are not really sure and, in some cases, have absolutely no idea what we are doing with this gift of life God gave us. We simply continue day by day. But, what if we would be truly willing to examine the character of the role we as individuals have chosen to play in our story? What if we would be willing to accept the challenge to turn around and face the back of this stage upon which we are all performing? What if we would agree to take a few steps back and, giving full attention, focus on the backdrop (which in this example would be toward the sky), then allow it to be slowly unzipped to unmask the greatest lie that Satan has used to deceive us to turn us away from God and witness the revealing of the real truth in the workmanship of "His story" (history), the tree of life?

The nucleus of life on earth was and still is family. The father is the head of the family. The sons and daughters are to worship and follow in the footsteps of the father. In the beginning, there was no mention of mother because mother or woman did not birth the first man. However, she was, from the beginning, created within *him*. That man was created by Almighty Father God. Genesis 1:27 (NKJV) says, "So God created man in His own image; in the image of God He created him; male and female He created them." Therefore, in the image of the Trinity the Almighty Father God, the Son of God, Jesus Christ, and the Holy Spirit He created them. Then God blessed the union of the two, to be fruitful and multiply and from there. the same two made us from the same image of the Trinity from which they were made.

Almighty God the Father, from whom we are to take our instruction, is the first person of the Trinity who, in regard to the way He created our bodies in their image, would be the innermost part of our body which would be represented by our bone. The bone, besides being the frame of the body, also houses the bone marrow, which manufactures stem cells and other substances that hold the body's instruction and information of how the Lord God created us. The bone marrow also produces blood cells according to the University of California, San Francisco, Benioff Children's Hospital in San Francisco. This means the bone marrow is the soil of the root from which the blood originates. The Bible tells us that the life of the flesh is in the blood (Leviticus 17:11 NKJV). The word *originate* means creation (Father God Elohim, the Creator). "The Lord is my rock and my fortress and my deliverer. My God, my strength in whom I will trust; my shield and the horn of my salvation, my stronghold" (Psalm 18:2 NKJV). The Rock. The foundation of man.

The second person of the Trinity. The Son of God the Father, Jesus Christ. "I and My Father are one" (John 10:30 NKJV). He, in regard to the way our bodies are created in their image, would represent the flesh we bear. Although there was no copulation, Jesus, the Son of the Father, was first the Word. Then that Word was spoken as light! Day! The light that overpowered the darkness of the deep! Then that Word became flesh by way of the virgin womb of a human female just as we did.

> In the beginning was the word, and the word was with God, and the word was God. (John 1:1 NKJV)
>
> And the word became flesh and dwelt among us, and we beheld His glory, the glory of the only begotten of the Father, full of grace and truth. (John 1:14 NKJV)

(The flesh. The outermost man. The visible God. Emanuel—God with us!)

And the third person of the Trinity, the Holy Spirit, the paraclete. The Holy Spirit is to God as a Wife is to a husband. The Bible addresses the Holy Spirit as a male as it is God's word because all life is created as male. The Father God is male. The Lord Jesus Christ, God's Son, is male. Adam, created from God the Father, is male. Woman that was pulled out of man is made from man, making her, "wo-man." A "female." Adam is he. Eve is she." Genesis 2:18 (NKJV) says, "And the Lord said, 'It is not good that man should be alone. I will make him a helper comparable to him.'" John 14:16–17 (NKJV) says, "And I will pray the Father, that He will give you another helper, that He may abide with you forever the Spirit of truth, whom the world cannot receive, because it neither sees Him or knows Him; but you know Him for He dwells with you and will be in you."

John 15:26 (NKJV) says, "But when the helper comes whom I shall send to you from the Father, the Spirit of Truth who proceeds from the Father, He will testify of me." This is not in any way to say that the power of the Holy Spirit is subservient or is not the whole power of the Almighty God because the Holy Spirit comes from God, but Jesus said, "The Spirit of Truth that proceeds from the Father," which means it is coming out of or being expelled from within the Father, just like woman came out of man. The Holy Spirit is the last of the Holy Trinity just as the woman is last to be made manifest in the creation of man in the image of the Trinity. God does not lie. If God said He created man in their likeness, in the likeness of the Trinity, and created woman within man as man's help, where is the image of the help within the Trinity?

The Holy Spirit is known as wonderful counselor, the comforter, the paraclete that lays parallel between the Father and the Son. The true witness is also called the helper. The Holy Spirit lays parallel to God, as woman lays parallel to man, as man lays parallel to Jesus Christ, and as Jesus Christ is parallel to the Father. Jesus answered, "Most assuredly, I say to you, unless one is born again of water and spirit, he cannot enter the kingdom of God. That which is born of flesh is flesh and arrives on earth through a human portal within water and blood. That which is born of spirit is spirit which arrives to earth from Heaven involving water baptism and baptism of the Holy Spirit. Do not marvel that I said to you, 'You must be born again'" (John 3:5–7 NKJV).

The woman holds the only portal on this earth by which the creation of human flesh can come from the hand of God in Heaven onto this earth (being born of the flesh). But because we are birthed into a world of sin and fallacy, the knowledge of evil finding its way to the soul of man made man unclean, taking man's heart away from God. But because Jesus Christ prayed of the Father to send another helper, that helper, the Holy Spirit, is the only one that can cleanse the unclean spirit (being born again but of the Holy Spirit). Believing and asking the Lord to come into your life and rule your life, having been baptized in water as a symbol of cleansing or purifying the body of the dirt and filth of the sin of this world and having been baptized of the Holy Spirit, is the only portal by which our renewed spirit can leave this unclean world and be returned to the hand of its rightful owner—the hand of our Father in Heaven.

It is the same notion as to wash your hands after they have become dirty. However, a water baptism is part of an eternal cleansing. So women, don't sell yourselves short by letting the world make you believe you have to fight to be equal to man financially or otherwise. If money is your god, then I can see where this might be a problem. But know that your place in this world can never be minimized because we have been given by God the power of the increase of man onto this earth. We, women, are truly blessed. We, through the seed of man, possess the ability of creation of all human vessels of which the spirit of God lives and functions, and that, blessed women, is priceless! So know who you are in Christ Jesus. Know who and what you were created to do and be. Man was created to worship, honor, praise and serve the one true God to fight and defeat the evil that was thrown down upon this earth and to love and cherish the woman that gives increase to the human vessels of God's army.

Woman was not created to create vessels of flesh to fill with the unholy spirit of evil. She was created to set upon this earth human vessels to be filled with the breath of the Almighty Father God. The Holy Spirit is the third and last mention of the Trinity in Heaven: the Father, the Son, and the Holy Spirit. The woman is the last mention of the Trinity on the earth: Jesus Christ, the man, and the woman. Remember earlier when the fetus in the womb was discussed? How in the sixth month of pregnancy the lungs of the fetus are fully developed but do not function? That is because the fetus is functioning off of the life source of its mother that keeps the fetus alive. Therefore, the fetus is alive because it continues to grow because of the life within the mother. However, in the womb or the matrix, it has not yet been given its spirit. When the fetus is released through the portal of its mother's womb and the doctor smacks the bottom of the fetus, the fetus is given and takes in its own breath gift of the spirit of life into its mouth and nostrils from the Father God, the same as of which Adam was given, which oxygenates the lungs that begin the creation of blood throughout the body by the movement of the Holy Spirit's breath of God who gives life.

Leviticus 17:14 says, "For it is the life of all flesh. The blood sustains its life. Therefore, I said to the children of Israel, 'You shall not eat the blood of any flesh, for the life of all flesh is in its blood. Whosoever eats it shall be cut off.'" As we all know and have seen in real life as well as television, when the skin of the vessel or human body is broken and the blood spills from it, we all know that if too much is lost, that death is inevitable. So I'm sorry to be the bearer of bad news, but the next time you speak of your child and say, "That child is my flesh and blood," that would only be partially incorrect. All children are of the flesh and bone of their parents by way of DNA. No child is given the blood from either parent. Each child's blood is determined by its first independent intake of oxygen through its nostrils, just as was given Adam, which makes each one of us a child of the Most High God. So don't allow Satan to trick you into thinking that the life inside the vessel of your child, which truly belongs to God the Father, came from you, because it did not. That vessel, the child's physical body, is of your DNA, but the life that is in the blood belongs to no one other than God To be granted this gift of being an inherent of God is the most absolute greatest gift available to man on this earth. However, with all of the evil that plagues this earth, it appears that darkness is making a strong comeback in the attempt to create total darkness. But because Jesus Christ is the light of this world and His light cannot be extinguished, even one child of God illuminated with His light will shine in that darkness. The more of God's children that seek and find that light and returns to it will cause the light of this world to grow larger and destroy that darkness, as we were created to do. That darkness that so desperately tries to darken us.

God has put truth of His Word and His love for us in such plain sight, and Satan does not want us to see it. His number one tactic is to create confusion. To him it is imperative that we follow in his direction than that of the Lord. If we could catch a glimpse of God's truth in motion, it just might be enough to wake us up or make us willing to give God a try. Well, here is a motion of God's truth. Have you ever been in a moving vehicle and a flock of birds, or even one for that matter, flew in front of your windshield and not one of them were destroyed? They may have sped up or diverted to the left or right, and some may have even flown under the vehicle. Or how all other life forms, in general, have the defense mechanisms they have but live in harmony with each other. They only kill out of their animal instinct for survival. Do you want to know why that is? The answer is simple and very true: they obeyed the command of their God. Their ancestors did not eat from the tree of knowledge of good and evil. We are the only ones of God's creation that did! We are the only ones of God's creation that is not in sync with our Creator. We are God's greatest creation, and we are the only ones out of order! Just think of the perfect harmony we could be living in had we obeyed God and not eaten from that tree. God told Adam first and foremost in Genesis 2:16, "And the Lord commanded man saying, 'Of every tree of the garden you may eat, but of the tree of the knowledge of good and evil you shall not eat, for in the day that you eat of it you shall surely die.'"

You see, from the very beginning God already established that this life He gives us is real, and we must lord over it at all times because God already knew that evil was here. He created us in His image and put His light of life in us to fight the evil He threw down that lives inside that darkness. That's why He created us in His image because God knew being anything less, we were not going to make it! God knew that Lucifer, after he became Satan, knew that too! Satan had already experienced the goodness of God while he was in Heaven, and later, jealousy developed within Satan a way to despise God's goodness and how to use it against God's creation. Immediately after God had created the opportunity for man to procreate, Satan took the opportunity to put his seed of darkness into the vessels of God's light, an act of getting a jump on God's power. Satan's plan was to take the vessels God created for God himself and use them to lessen the light of God that is intended to destroy Satan's darkness. That is why those two trees were in the garden of Eden and Eden only, because Eden was a land in Heaven where Satan dwelled and darkened.

The tree of life is a representation of eternal life. When God pulled earth out of Heaven and earth became new, that new birth was the baptism of Eden. Anything that becomes new in God has to experience a physical cleansing. The earth was fertile and the garden was not dark and desolate, not until man failed God and God cursed the land. It is interesting that the Lord uses the tree in His visual of life and death. A tree is a lot stronger than it looks and can continue to live as long as its root is deeply planted in good soil and fresh water. Symbolically the tree of life as life was intended, the earth was alive and fertile. The root of the tree of life was deeply planted with life in that God created earth. That life endowed root or foundation sprouts up the strong and sturdy trunk, which serves as the body or flesh of the tree. That trunk births the limbs or *sons and daughters* of the tree, and the limbs sprout the leaves or *fruits* of the generation. of life throughout.

The two trees in the garden represents the two kingdoms on earth. The tree of life represents the life God intended us to have and how to have it more abundantly. The tree of the good life. The tree of eternal life. So no matter which road or branch we may have taken, or wherever we might be on that tree, life within that particular tree would not let us down. From top to bottom, left to right, limb to limb, and leaf to leaf, as long as we ate from that tree, we would have lived with the surety and confidence of unity with God. Because we would live for God. He would be our sustenance, and we would have been in sync with His will for us. But because we have bypassed that opportunity of life and chose to eat from the tree of knowledge of good and evil, on this earth we will never know what life would have been like, because although God has forgiven us, oftentimes we don't know how to forgive ourselves, nor forget the wrong we've done. Nevertheless, the tree of life is the life God intended us to have.

Therefore, we have no one to blame but ourselves. But the good news is God has given us a way out if we are willing to accept it. God gave us a Savior whose name is Jesus Christ, Emanuel, "God with us," who sacrificed His only begotten Son and allowed His blood to be shed to pay for the sins of our life because we were created to be one family. Created in the image of one God, one begotten Son, and one Holy Spirit.

God created us in their image and the Image God created us in is Holy. It is the Holy image of family. The Father (husband) as the head, power and or nucleus of the family. The direction the rest of the family is to follow. (The Holy family.) The Holy Spirit, also known as the counselor, advocate, paraclete, help or Bride (wife) of God. The Holy Spirit lays parallel between the Father and Son (child/ren,) The Holy Spirit is among other things, The Grace of God. The Holy Spirit is not the image of The Holy Spirit. The Holy Spirit is not as a human woman who is sought after her curves and carnality because The Holy Spirit is not of flesh but is the love, the helper and softer side of God who Keeps the law, peace and advocates for Gods family. She is also called Grace. Proverbs 18:22 says "He who finds a wife finds a good thing and obtains favor from the Lord. And the Lord Jesus Christ who is the Child of God that became flesh, who does the work of the Father and is filled with forgiveness, peace and grace from the Holy Spirit. So, if anyone tells you that God needs nothing to be who He is, is somewhat of an oxymoron, because God is God all by Himself, He has to be made Himself, of the images in which He made us. One Heavenly Father, one Son, one Holy Spirit. One earthly father, one earthly mother and one child, or however many children enter the family, you still end up with ONE family, being who and what it is, all by itself. Take a look at yourself and, if you are fortunate enough to have them, take a look at your wife and child(ren), can you honestly say they are not a portion of the sum of what makes you who (the one person) you are?

All we have to do is thank the Lord for His sacrifice, take His hand, surrender the rest of our life to His hand, and walk out of that darkness. And when you do, as you are lifted away from the Sins of tree of the knowledge of good and evil, just know that Satan will try to hold you back, but just concentrate on the fact that you've given your life to a higher and far stronger power than the one trying to hold you back. It will eventually make you stronger in Christ and teach you how to begin to fly like a bird on the wings of the Lord because He has taken all of the burden of our sins and have cast them into the deepest part of the sea that they will never pass across His mind again so that the pressure of our life may be lifted away and start life anew.

So, in conclusion, let it be made known that the stage upon which the Lord God Almighty produces and directs is not the system of this world which is behind the zipper but the system that is in front of it!

Because the Word of God and all that is within it comes from Heaven! So don't get it twisted. Looking from Heaven's view, the stage of the world down here would be compared to that of the fictional land of Oz. But in the real world, in the Heaven that stands before this world, I believe our Father who art in Heaven is saying, "Pay no attention to the one behind the curtain! Because I Am that I Am, the one true God. I am your Father in Heaven. And there's no place like home!"

Spreadin' the News
My Song

I'm spreadin' the news, it's gonna be grand!Don't you want
to be a part of it?
He's coming again!
He once came to this world to give

His life so we may live,
abundant in life, in paradise,
when His kingdom comes.

I'm spreadin' the news, He's calling your name.
No matter how you've lived your life,
misfortuned or famed.
His salvation you can trust, He'll only ask that you must,
Believe in His life, the fact that He died,
And now lives again!
If you want to feel the love of Christ,
just give Him your life, then you've done what's best.
And as you choose to be a part, give Him all your heart,
He'll do the rest!

He's waiting for you to call on His name.
He knows you want to change your life, though you may
feel ashamed. He'll replace your sins with grace,
Consume you in His embrace. The Shepherd is bound
To search till one is found, His love that was lost.

And if you'll just meet Him there, you can go
anywhere,
In Christ our Lord, in Christ our Lord.
(August, 2011. Revised February 18, 2019)

Written by Wanda F. Kenty

Munchies for the Mind

For those of you who, after all you have read, still believe there is no God, or may believe there is something out there but you don't need it or you can take care of yourself and can find your own answers to all of your own questions, then I wonder if you can help me out.

I have questions of my own that, for as long as they have been "on my plate," so to speak, I have not been able to answer. I call them "Munchies for the Mind." They are wondrous bits of thought that my mind chews on from time to time. These particular two munchies, even though they appear to be bite-sized thoughts, are still too big for the stomach of my understanding to digest. Here goes.

While in silence I think to myself, how is it possible for the mind to speak to you, but the mind has no tongue? And, how is it possible for you to hear what the mind is saying, while the mind has no voice?

You can't escape the power of the voice of God, no matter who tries to interrupt the conversation. To whom do you lend your ear?

By the *grace* of God.

We are fearfully and wonderfully made!

The price of life is love
And right or wrong results its dues.
What determines your life's balance is
Your ability to choose. (1990)

Written by Wanda F. Kenty

APPENDIX
THE MESOAMERICAN SACRUM BONE: DOORWAY TO THE OTHERWORLD

Brian Stross

Abstract

This study links body symbolism, religious experience, and visual representation through a consideration of the sacrum bone and the surrounding pelvic girdle in cosmological traditions of Mesoamerica. An argument is put forward, using ethnographic, linguistic, and iconographic evidence, that the sacrum bone was a "sacred" bone, that it played a significant part in some pre-Hispanic Mesoamerican iconographic and cosmological traditions as it did in some Old World cultures, that it was related to reproduction, fertility, and reincarnation, and that in Mesoamerica the sacrum represented one index of the more generalized but variously manifested "portals" or doorways permitting translocation of shamans, spirits, and deities between worlds or levels of the cosmos.

Introduction

The human body is sometimes referred to as the "sacred vessel," and various parts of the body play their parts in the observance of religious ritual, retaining through tradition different kinds of symbolic significance; whether it is hands folded in prayer or making the sign of the cross, a tongue receiving the host or pronouncing the name of

92

a Saint, or a heart brocaded on a priestly garment or wrested from the chest of a sacrificial victim with the assistance of obsidian knives. The body, its parts and functions and its symbolism function both to manifest signals of social differentiation in culture and to interpret them, creating social structure and cosmological models underlying it (Lopez Austin 1988; Houston et al 2006). The ancient Maya, like their modem descendants, attached great importance to the human skull, and even the lower jawbone of an animal alone is believed by many Indigenous Mesoamericans to be connected to the animal's spiritual essence (Foster 1945). The ritual and symbolic importance of the body and its parts is illustrated here, not with hands or hearts or jawbones, but by a case study of the cultural symbolism and ritual meanings in Mesoamerica of a less frequently considered body part, the sacrum.

In Mesoamerica the sacrum, along with closely associated bones, is apparently seen as sacred in some Indigenous societies even today, though surely less so now than in earlier times. The name "sacrum," designating the more or less flat bone with eight holes located at the base of the spine, comes directly from Latin *os sacrum*, meaning 'sacred bone'. Sugar points out that while most bone names readily reveal their origins, it has long been a mystery why the sacrum bone (*os sacrum*) should be called the "holy bone." "That it is a translation from the Greek *hieron osteon* merely pushes the inquiry back from the first Latin use in about 400 AD to the time of Hippocrates (about 400 BC) (1987:2061). Following the trail through several explanatory hypotheses about the origins of the name sacrum, Sugar introduces evidence that the sacrum in tradition was the bone necessary for resurrection, identifying it as the "almond" OTIUZ of the Hebrews and the *ajb* of the Arabs, and ultimately deriving its conceptual underpinnings from the ancient Egyptians (1987:2062-2063).

Upon finding that some Mesoamerican Indian languages also named this bone with words referring to sacredness and deity, one may well ask why societies distant from one another refer to the sacrum as a "sacred" or "holy" bone. Presumably such naming practices reflect independently, rather than through diffusion, the cultural importance of this bone, and one can suggest plausible explanations, based, on observational logic, for its being termed "sacred." The word "sacred" for our purposes can be defined as "worthy of veneration, reverence, and respect on the one hand, and protected by tradition and ritual against symbolic or actual abuse on the other."

The sacrum bone is, among other things, the fulcrum of support for the human torso, and as such is well designed to take great physical stress. It is what we sit on, and by sitting we place ourselves at rest in a position that can be maintained without significant movement for long periods of time. Perhaps more importantly from perspectives of symbolism and cultural importance, it is located next to the reproductive organs, which are of utmost significance for the species as well as the individual, and are surely of great significance in most if not all societies. In its proximal location, the sacrum could well be thought to share significant qualities with the reproductive organs, and even to transport material from the brain to those organs.

Several cultures around the world assume that the sacrum participates directly in procreation by channeling seminal fluid through die spinal column to the penis, most notably ancient Egyptians and some cultures of India. Its location on the body and the formal similarity of spinal fluid to semen provide an observational basis for these conclusions. Even Leonardo da Vinci, with such a fine grasp of human anatomy, must have made a similar assumption, for he placed in his drawing of a human male a seminal duct leading from the sacrum at the bottom of the spinal cord to the penis (Huxley 1974:64).

Sacredness of this bone is also related to a belief found in various parts of the globe that the sacrum is the "resurrection bone" from which residual raw material remaining after death a person will be reborn, presumably by attracting the spirit residing within. This notion may spring from the observation that as an especially hard bone, the sacrum resists disintegration through time, and is often among the very last visible remains of a body that has been left on the ground or that has been unearthed long after burial. A rational basis for attaching importance to the sacrum bone can thus be constructed from empirical observations and conclusions underlain by a kind of observational logic.

Evidence of human use of the sacrum goes back perhaps as much as eighteen thousand years in Mexico, to one of the earliest evidences of art in the New World; the carved sacrum of a now extinct camel-like animal, found on the banks of Lake Texcoco in the Valley of Mexico (Figure 1)2. Retrieved in 1870 from some forty feet below the surface, this artifact was worked into the form of an animal skull, perhaps representing a deer, or a dog (cf. Weaver 1981:28). One might even suppose that it was intended to represent the skull of the particular extinct camelid from which the sacrum bone was taken. Based on argument presented below, one could also contend that the choice of the sacrum bone for this depiction of an animal head or skull was quite deliberate, made precisely because it was a sacrum bone and not some other bone or material.

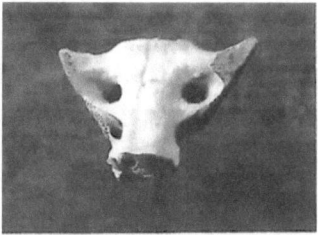

Figure 1 Sacrum of extinct camelid carved to represent a mammal's skull, fits the Mesoamerican notion of the sacrum as a second "skull" (photograph courtesy of Instituto Nacional de Antropologia e Historia, Mexico)

Consistent with ethnographically documented traditions in Mesoamerica, and with interpretations concerning sacrum associated symbolism, the sacrum's carvers may have believed it to house some spiritual essence of a hunted animal—an essence perhaps traditionally thought to be simultaneously located in an Otherworld Ritual care for the bone would have been, among other reasons, ideologically motivated to ensure success in the hunt and favor of the gods, based on intentions of not angering the Master of Animals nor the spirits of the animals themselves, to use an analogy from some current traditions (see e.g. Foster 1945:186; Alcorn 1984:88; Parsons 1936:48; Lipp 1991:95).

In Mesoamerica today ceremonial masks are sometimes made from animal pelvic bones, and Cordry believes the camelid sacrum mentioned above was probably also used as a mask in front of the face (1980:79-80). This suggests the possibility that some Mesoamericans have noticed the resemblance between the skull and the pelvic girdle, between the head and the pelvis. More direct evidence on this point is available. During fieldwork with Tzeltal Mayans of highland Chiapas, Mexico I was told that the human body has two "skulls" (*bakeltik*)—one at the top of the spine *(bakel hol)* and one at the bottom (*bakel kub*) and that these skulls are connected by a "serpent" (chan) which I take to mean the spinal cord or the vertebral column (Figure 2).3 The two skulls are sacred, and ritually important because they are seen to contain the essence of a person. The most sacred points of the body are the mouth or the top of head (at the fontanel), and the base of the spine, because through these paths the soul enters and leaves the body.4 Related concepts have been articulated by Huastec (Teenek) Mayans to Alcorn, though without specific mention of the hip region (1984:67).

ABOUT THE AUTHOR

Wanda Kenty was born a seventh child of a seventh child. During her childhood and throughout her teenage years she was engaged in an on and off search for God but could not find him. She had made so many mistakes during that time, that her life just did not make sense anymore. She didn't know what to do to get God's attention. So, one day she opened her heart to God and cried out to him to show his face. She told him, she needed him! But she didn't know how to have faith in him. She told him she once heard that faith comes by hearing, and hearing by the word of God. So, she told God she was going to close her eyes, open her bible and ask God to take her to a place in his word where she could see what faith looks like. So, she closed her eyes and placed her fingers in the bible. When she felt to stop, she opened the bible. And there before her eyes was…

The 23rd Psalm. A very true story. When she finally learned to surrender, she didn't have to search anymore. God came to her.

www.ingramcontent.com/pod-product-compliance
Lightning Source LLC
Chambersburg PA
CBHW020319130626
46549CB00003B/937